CONTENTS

To the Members of the First Baptist Church of Waco

I am grateful for the love and support you have given to me
as the words and thoughts in this book have been formed.
It is wonderful to walk the pathway
of Christian discipleship together.

FOOTSTEPS OF THE FISHERMAN

With St. Peter on the Path of Discipleship

SCOTT WALKER

Augsburg Books
MINNEAPOLIS

FOOTSTEPS OF THE FISHERMAN
With St. Peter on the Path of Discipleship

Scripture taken from the New American Standard Bible ®, Copyright © 1960,
1962, 1963, 1968, 1971, 1972, 1973, 1975, 1977, 1995 by The Lockman
Foundation. Used by permission.

Large-quantity purchases or custom editions of this book are available at a dis-
count from the publisher. For more information, contact the sales department at
Augsburg Fortress, Publishers, 1-800-328-4648, or write to: Sales Director,
Augsburg Fortress, Publishers, P.O. Box 1209, Minneapolis, MN 55440-1209.

ISBN 0-8066-3724-2

Cover design by Marti Naughton
Book design by Michelle L. N. Cook and Abby Coles
Cover art from Art Resource: Burnand, Eugene (1850-1921)
The Apostles Saint Peter and John Rushing to the Sepulchre. Musee d'Orsay, Paris,
France. Photo credit : Giraudon

The paper used in this publication meets the minimum requirements of
American National Standard for Information Sciences—Permanence of Paper for
Printed Library Materials, ANSI Z329.48-1984. ♾ ™

Manufactured in the U.S.A.

07   06   05   04   3   4   5   6   7   8   9   10

INTRODUCTION

SEVERAL WEEKS AGO I WAS TEACHING A BIBLE STUDY ON THE APOSTLE Paul's Epistle to the Philippians. As we moved into the final chapter of the epistle, I could picture the old apostle gearing up for a stirring conclusion. Perhaps while pacing a jailhouse floor in Rome as he dictated his letter, he stopped, took a deep breath, and thrusting a long ex-Pharisee's forefinger into the air, lost himself in a flow of words:

> Finally, brethren, whatever is true, whatever is honorable, whatever is right, whatever is pure, whatever is lovely, whatever is of good repute, if there is any excellence and if anything worthy of praise, dwell on these things. The things you have learned and received and heard and seen in me, practice these things, and the God of peace will be with you. (4:8–9)

Now, I am not criticizing Paul, but when I read Paul's words, I immediately felt guilty and thought to myself: "I could never say that. I could never look out at these good folks sitting around these prayer meeting tables and tell them to practice the things they have seen in me. I am just not that confident and sure of myself."

I guess the truth is that while I do try to lead by example, I am also conscious of my faults and weaknesses. Granted, most of my struggles are hidden under a thin veneer of politeness and professional gentility. But if people could know me like I know myself, they would see a lot of faults, weaknesses, and struggles. I am a Christian disciple who barely cuts the mustard on many days.

I think that many of you who read these words know what I am talking about. Most of us hang on to our Christian character by bloodied fingernails. And we have probably learned far more about faith from our glaring failures than we have from our stellar victories. We try to be good examples of Christ-likeness, and many times we succeed. But about the moment we make the All Saints Dean's List, we trip and find ourselves sitting on our humble fannies again.

I guess this is why two contrasting apostolic giants are prominently depicted in the early history of the New Testament Church. One is the Apostle Paul, who, though open with his faults, is depicted as leading by vigorous and positive example. On the other hand, we have the Apostle Peter—

equally prominent and respected—who is depicted as leading despite recurrent failure and struggle. Perhaps there is a reason for this.

Allow me to tell you a little-known story from scattered pages of the New Testament. I will present the story in an abbreviated outline for now. However, if this footnote from history pricks your curiosity, you will find it recounted in greater detail in an appendix at the end of this book. This is a story about the man who is most likely responsible for preserving and depicting the personality of the Apostle Peter, John Mark of Jerusalem.

John Mark was born in Jerusalem near the time of Jesus' death. John Mark's mother, Mary, was a Christian, and her spacious home was used as a meeting place for early Christians. As a young boy, John Mark knew the Apostle Peter because he was likely a frequent visitor in his mother's home. Later, after Peter and his wife had been forced to flee from Jerusalem for their lives, John Mark also was introduced to the Apostle Paul, through his cousin Barnabas.

When John Mark was a young man, he accompanied Paul and Barnabas on a portion of Paul's first missionary journey. Years later John Mark ended up in Rome, serving as an assistant to the Apostle Paul, who was under house arrest, and as a personal secretary to the Apostle Peter, who was a leader in the Roman Church.

In A.D. 64–65, the Roman emperor Nero instigated the first great persecution against the Christians in Rome. Though John Mark survived the holocaust, both the Apostles Peter and Paul were likely martyred. In the midst of the death of these great leaders, John Mark recognized a need to write a book that recorded some of the earliest Christians' memories of the life and ministry of Jesus. The book that emerged from John Mark's writing is what we know today as the Gospel of Mark, the first of the Gospels to be written.

As John Mark wrote this short account, he was determined to develop the theme of *the struggle of Christian discipleship.* John Mark looked at his fellow Christians in Rome in the midst of persecution, and realized that to be a Christian is a most difficult challenge. Many had seen loved ones tortured and killed because they would not renounce their faith. Others were dealing with gnawing guilt because they had renounced their faith—they had shouted, "I do not believe in Jesus Christ!"—to protect their families and survive another day. Now many who had remained loyal and paid dearly for their faith would not forgive their brothers and sisters who had recanted. Faced with such difficult times and events, John Mark decided that a primary theme in his Gospel would be that *it is only through struggle and personal failure that we grow stronger in our faith and in our understanding of Jesus.* To paraphrase the writing of Ernest Hemingway, it seems that as Christians we only grow *stronger in the broken places.*

To develop this theme, John Mark chose a well-known character who had the greatest respect of Roman Christians. He selected the martyred Apostle Peter, a man he knew intimately. Through his writing John Mark brought Peter center stage in the Gospel story, often relating how the great fisherman frequently failed, but was ultimately true to his calling. Through the Apostle Peter, John Mark allowed struggling Roman Christians to learn important lessons concerning Christian discipleship. He enabled them to keep alive the hope that though they had failed grievously, they too could rise from their despair and follow Jesus as Peter had.

I guess this is why I have always identified so well with the Apostle Peter in the Gospels. He is the one character on the Gospel stage who acts the most like me. And I take courage from his very human example. I frequently think, "If Peter can succeed despite his glaring faults and weaknesses, maybe I can too."

The purpose of this book is to isolate various stories that are told about Peter in the Gospels and in the Acts of the Apostles. As we study each story, we will ask the questions: How does Simon Peter's predicament apply to my life? What can I learn through Peter's experience that will make me a better Christian disciple? I believe that these are the questions that John Mark and the other Gospel writers intended for us to ask. So without further ado, let's set forth on a journey with the Apostle Peter as he seeks to follow Jesus and grows in faith and maturity. From Peter's life, let's glean lessons pertaining to Christian discipleship. We'll begin with discovering how Peter met Jesus in the first place.

Reflections

For a righteous man falls seven times, and rises again.
  —*Proverbs 24:16*

It is the true nature of mankind to learn from mistakes, not from examples.
  —*Fred Hoyle*[1]

He who has never failed somewhere, that man cannot be great.
  —*Herman Melville*[2]

The credit belongs to the man who is actually in the arena; whose face is marred by dust and sweat and blood; who strives valiantly; who errs and comes short again and again; who knows the great enthusiasm, the great devotions, and spends himself in a worthy cause; who, at best, knows in the end the triumph of high achievement; and who at the worst, if he fails, at

least fails while daring greatly, so that his place shall never be with those cold and timid souls who know neither victory nor defeat.
—*Theodore Roosevelt*[3]

The world breaks every one and afterward many are strong at the broken places.
—*Ernest Hemingway*[4]

Dear Father,

As I embark on this study of the life of Simon Peter, may I see within his personality the reflection of my own nature, the depth of my own soul. May I learn through his struggles that I too will fall prey to evil and must learn to trust your forgiving grace. Help me to know that without being broken I cannot grow strong. And that without personal defeat, I cannot experience the ultimate victory that comes through the strength of Christ alone. May I learn through these pages important lessons in Christian discipleship. Amen.

Chapter One

FIRST IMPRESSIONS

Again the next day John was standing with two of his disciples, and he looked at Jesus as He walked, and said, "Behold, the Lamb of God!" The two disciples heard him speak, and they followed Jesus. And Jesus turned, and saw them following, and said to them, "What do you seek?" They said to Him, "Rabbi (which translated means Teacher), where are You staying?" He said to them, "Come, and you will see." So they came and saw where He was staying; and they stayed with Him that day, for it was about the tenth hour [4 P. M.]. One of the two who heard John speak and followed Him, was Andrew, Simon Peter's brother. He found first his own brother Simon, and said to him, "We have found the Messiah" (which translated means Christ). He brought him to Jesus. Jesus looked at him and said, "You are Simon the son of John; you shall be called Cephas (which is translated Peter). (John 1:35-42)

THERE COMES A TIME IN OUR ADULTHOOD WHEN MANY OF US MEET Jesus as if for the first time. We may have been professing Christians for years. We may have worn out our shoes walking to and from church. But there comes a moment—perhaps many moments—when suddenly we are introduced to Jesus in an entirely new way. Typically this introduction comes through the catalyst of an experience that forces us to view Jesus as we never have before. Inevitably, through this new introduction, we gain an insight into ourselves that is also novel. For a moment, let us look at the first time Peter came face-to-face with a young carpenter from Nazareth named Jesus. Let's begin with a brief sketch of Peter's early life.

THE FIRST MENTION OF SIMON PETER IN THE GOSPEL RECORD IS NOT found in the Gospel of Mark but rather in the Gospel of John. John alone saves for us the memory of how Peter was introduced to Jesus by Peter's brother, Andrew.

What little we know about Peter prior to this scene is sketchy. John 1:44 relates that Peter and Andrew were originally from the small Galilean fishing village of Bethsaida, which was also the hometown of the Apostle Philip. Bethsaida does not exist today, but archaeological evidence reveals that the village was positioned on the northeastern bank of the Jordan River, at the point where the Jordan empties into the northern tip of the Sea of Galilee. Appropriately, *Bethsaida* means "Fisherman's City."

We can assume several things about Peter's childhood. First, Peter was probably bilingual. Most men involved in trade and commerce in Galilee worked in an environment that was both Jewish and Greek. This cultural pluralism is evidenced by the fact that Peter's brother, Andrew, bears a Greek name, and even Peter's given name, Simon, is a Greek derivative.

Though Acts 4:13 states that Peter was regarded as being "uneducated and untrained," it is unlikely that he was illiterate. Most Jewish boys received a simple education through the village synagogue. Such an education would have given Peter knowledge of important portions of Jewish scripture, perhaps the ability to read, and an introduction to basic mathematics.

We can also assume that at an early age, Peter began as an apprentice to his father, to learn his trade as a fisherman. Most men followed their father's profession. It would have also been customary for Peter to have been married during his teenage years.

As Peter walks onto the gospel stage, he is a young married man, has moved from Bethsaida to the fishing village of Capernaum on the northwestern shore of the Sea of Galilee, and is living with his mother-in-law (Mark 1:29-30). Whether Peter and his wife had children is unknown.

To Follow Jesus Is an Intentional Decision

The story begins with the stern and severe character of John the Baptist. John is a relative of Jesus', most likely a cousin.[1] Standing on the fringe of the desert, John thunders like an ancient prophet, nipping at the heels of a spiritually wayward Israel, calling them to repentance and accountability to God. As if in a theater, John the Baptist walks to the center of the Gospel stage and announces that the lights are dimming, the curtain is going up, and people had better be quiet and listen to Jesus.

This young, eccentric prophet dressed in camelskin rags was tired of Jews assuming that they were children of God—God's chosen people—simply because they had been biologically born as Jews. By taking their religious heritage for granted, many Jews had forgotten that their relationship to God was not based on heredity, nationality, and tradition, but on personally loving God and obeying his commandments. The result, in John's opinion, was that Israel was not being loyal to God and living as the nation that God intended.

To call his fellow Jews back into an acceptable relationship with God, John did a radical and symbolic thing. He invited his fellow Jews to participate in *proselyte baptism*. What is proselyte baptism, and what does it symbolize?

Often Gentiles, non-Jews such as Roman soldiers, would visit Palestine and become interested in the God of the Jews. Many began to believe in this great Jewish God. If a Gentile adopted the beliefs of a Jew, he would be called a *God Fearer*. However, if a Gentile became so devoted to the God of Abraham that he literally wanted to become a Jew, then he—and it could only be a male—would have to do three things: 1) become circumcised, 2) promise to give alms to the Temple, and 3) undergo proselyte baptism, wherein his whole body would be ritually immersed in water for the purpose of spiritual purification. If these three requirements were accomplished, then a Gentile could become a Jew.

What John the Baptist was doing that was so radical (indeed, scandalous) was to ask Jews, not Gentiles, to undergo proselyte baptism. What he in effect was saying was: "My Jewish brothers, you cannot be a child of God by heredity or nationality. You can be a child of God only through personal decision and individual commitment. Come, repent of your sins, and symbolize your obedience to God through baptism."

Of course, most Jews were insulted by John's preaching, if they took it seriously at all. But Andrew, Simon Peter's brother, had become a disciple of John the Baptist. He accepted the fiery young prophet's words as truth. And perhaps Simon did as well.

All of the Gospel writers concur that Jesus of Nazareth agreed with what his kinsman John was saying. And because he agreed that a relationship with God is a personal decision, he symbolized his agreement by asking John to baptize him. It was in this moment that Andrew met Jesus and was attracted to him.

Christian discipleship always begins when we accept personal responsibility for our own spiritual life, realizing that it is not the traditions of our family, culture, or nation that make us Christians, but our individual decision to become a child of God.

My parents were both devout Christians. They read Bible stories to me from the time I could first understand words. Every meal was preceded by a prayer of thanksgiving. There was rarely a Sunday when my family did not go to church. Christianity was a central part of my family and cultural tradition.

Yet there came a time—indeed, there have been many times—when I have had to decide for myself whether or not I am a Christian. I remember my college years, when I finally escaped from under my parent's firm thumb. I discovered that I much preferred to sleep in on Sunday mornings rather than worship God with other Christians. I also remember the intellectual struggles of those years, when I could no longer believe in God simply because my mother and father did. I had to find my own intellectual reasons for belief and obedience. Though all of this seemed both liberating and threatening to me, it was necessary in order to make my own decision as to whether or not I truly was a Christian.

Somewhere in adulthood a Christian disciple moves from being a Christian because of tradition to becoming a Christian by conviction.

Our Desire Is to Be at Home with God

On a pivotal day that shaped human history, John the Baptist pointed a bony finger toward Jesus and informed Andrew and an unnamed disciple that he thought Jesus was God's promised Messiah. To use John's ancient terminology, he had become convinced that Jesus was "the Lamb of God who takes away the sin of the world" (John 1:29, 36). Exactly what John meant by these ancient words is not certain. Perhaps John was not even sure. But John had spiritual intuition that his kinsman had an incredible role to play in the spiritual history of Israel. And he told Andrew so.

Impressed, Andrew and the unnamed disciple began to trudge up the path after Jesus. Seeing them, Jesus stopped and turned, and an interesting conversation ensued. Jesus asked a pointed question, "What do you seek?" or "Why are you following me?"

In response, Andrew and his friend blurted out a curious reply: "Where are You staying?"

Without answering their question—and perhaps with a wry smile on his lips—Jesus simply said, "Come, and you will see." Following him further, they arrived at Jesus' lodging late in the afternoon and probably spent the night. Their conversation is sadly lost to history.

This is a simple story, but it is a story that must be seen on two levels: the factual and the symbolic. Within the short, pithy conversation between Jesus, Andrew, and the unnamed friend—possibly the author of the Gospel of John—the spiritual wellspring for Christian discipleship is found.

When Jesus turns to Andrew and his friend and asks them, "What do you seek?" he is asking this question to everyone who would consider following him as a disciple. It is a deep existential question. What is it that we seek most in life? What is it that sends us off on a spiritual quest for God? Why do we want to follow Jesus?

Perhaps the answer is intimated in Andrew's awkward, half-baked, spontaneous reply: "Where are you staying?" In these innocent, timid, searching words are found the heartbeat of the human soul. Above all, most people want to know where God is. We are spiritually lonely. We want to know where Ultimate Truth is so that we might find it, know it, understand it, and experience it. Quite simply, when our vision is purest and our minds most clear, we desire with all our heart to be "at home" with God, to stay with God, to abide in him.

St. Augustine struggled to convey this same spiritual truth in the fourth century, amid his own searching and loneliness. In the most quoted statement in his *Confessions,* he cries out, "Thou hast made us for Thyself and our heart is restless until it rests in thee."[2]

This is what Andrew meant—perhaps without even knowing it—when, confronted by Jesus' probing question, he blurts out, "Rabbi, where are You staying?" Andrew wanted to know more than a street address or the name of a country inn. For John the Baptist had told Andrew—more by the fire in his eyes and the tone of his voice than by his opaque words—that this Jesus of Nazareth was the man who could lead him to God.

This is where Christian discipleship begins, not out of family tradition or cultural values, but when we develop a hunger and thirst to "know where God is staying." It begins when life has knocked us down, beat us up, made us homesick in a far-off land, and we long with all our heart to be at home with our Father. It begins with an aching in our soul so strong that we are willing to follow Jesus "to where he is staying." We will make that unknown journey.

I have a close friend who grew up in a traditional Christian home. As a teenager he began to distance himself from God, though God never distanced himself from my friend. He was an outstanding athlete and went to a major university on a football scholarship. His life became one vast party filled with emptiness.

One night he went to a rock concert and overdosed on a concoction of drugs. Sitting in a dark arena filled with smoke and blasting music, he felt his chest begin to throb with pain; his breath grew short, and he knew that he was on the verge of cardiac arrest. Slowly he stood up and staggered outside into the coolness of the night. The pain began to abate. But reality and fear crashed in on him. Like a lost child, he desperately longed to go home.

Slowly he recovered and within an hour began to walk frantically toward his parents' home in another city, thirty miles away. Hitching rides, he traveled all night. But he made it home. Safely home.

Out of the depths of this traumatic experience, he began to read his Bible and to pray again. He began to search for God. He wanted to know where Jesus was staying in his world. Gradually he was reintroduced to Jesus. With the same wry grin on his face, Jesus said to him, "Come, and you will see."

Most of our experiences are not so dramatic. But all of us who are Christian disciples come to the point when we want to know where Jesus is staying. We want to be with him and learn from him. We want to be brought into the loving presence of God.

Introduced to a Jesus We Do Not Know

Andrew's first reaction after meeting Jesus was to go and find his brother, Simon, and share his exciting news with him. Whether or not Simon was also a disciple of John the Baptist we do not know. But Simon, working side by side with his brother as fishermen, certainly had heard plenty about John and his radical religious views. Now Simon was hearing his wide-eyed brother proclaiming, "We have found the Messiah!"

Perhaps Simon shared his brother's excitement, or perhaps he shook his head in disbelief. But when Andrew exclaimed the word *Messiah,* Simon certainly was expecting someone different from Jesus. When Simon heard the word *Messiah,* he would naturally think of the words *politics* and *power.* The Messiah, though perhaps disguised to evade the Romans, would become a super King David, who, empowered by God, would crush the Roman Army, give the people of Israel their freedom, and elevate their nation to a superpower. Then Israel could reign supreme as God's chosen people. Simon wanted to meet such a man.

In this encounter we see two truths emerge about people who are introduced to Jesus. First, they are usually introduced by a caring person—not by a book, a Gospel tract, a television evangelist, or a radio show. It is usually somebody that they know and trust.

My friend who overdosed at the rock concert was introduced to Jesus by his university football team's chaplain. Returning to college after his brush with death, my friend sought out the chaplain. Slowly, over a number of days, the chaplain began to share with him about his own struggles for faith, his own failures, and how his relationship with Jesus Christ had helped him overcome these things. Because my friend trusted the chaplain, he was willing to be introduced to Jesus, to give Jesus a chance to bring sanity and hope back into his frazzled life.

All of us need an Andrew to introduce us to Jesus. And we in turn can be an Andrew for others. There is no substitute for a friendship that spans the distance between Jesus and one who does not know him.

A second truth that emerges from the introduction of Simon to Jesus is that most of us initially come into a friendship with Jesus with distorted ideas and misconceptions. Simon would believe for the next three years that Jesus really would pull it out in the end and become a political hero. It was only when Simon was thrust face-to-face with the gruesome realities of Jesus' crucifixion, and then the mind-blowing experience of the resurrection, that Simon was ready to understand that Jesus was a totally different kind of Messiah than he expected and demanded; that he was, indeed, the "Son of God."

New Christians (and experienced Christians!) can have some unrealistic expectations, selfish motivations, and distorted theology when they first meet

Jesus. But that is where we all must start. It is only in following Jesus for a long time that we begin to understand who Jesus really is—and who he is not.

When I first began to follow Jesus, I honestly believed that if I prayed for something hard enough and often enough, my prayer would be answered. I remember the day that my father was rushed to a hospital with a massive heart attack. I prayed as earnestly as I could that his life would be spared. But he died before he ever saw a doctor.

To say the least, this jolted my fledgling theology. I wanted a Messiah who could stop bullets, cure cancer, rescue my father from a heart attack, and make my world a safer place to live. Jolted by my father's death, I had to shake my head and realize that I didn't have all the nice, neat answers that I wanted. And I gradually realized that I couldn't shape Jesus into my own image of a Messiah.

But slowly there was resurrection. Over decades I have come to understand that God is much bigger than death. And that God is much bigger than me and my limited understanding and naive expectations. As a teenager I began to follow a Jesus who was different from what I could ever have anticipated. And I am still in the process of learning who Jesus is.

Andrew introduced Simon to Jesus in a way that only a brother can do, and Simon, perhaps full of hope, gazed curiously at Jesus. Simon could never have believed in that moment how this introduction would totally change his life.

The Jesus Who Sees the Real Me   Ps. 139

Simon may not have had the first clue to who Jesus was. But Jesus knew intimately who Simon was. Looking deeply into the rough-hewn core of the man, Jesus gazed at him with warm humor in his eyes and said, "You are Simon the son of John; you shall be called Cephas."

Jesus was affectionately giving Peter a nickname. *Cephas* means "rock" in Hebrew. And *Cephas* is translated as "Petros" in Greek. And *Petros* is translated as "Peter" in English. Jesus saw something of great, solid strength in this young fisherman. He identified that strength and gave it a name: Peter, the Rock.

Many of us have not yet identified our greatest strengths. We do not have the ability—or have not been thrust into the galvanizing situation—to see and understand our God-given abilities. To follow Jesus is to be sent on a lifelong journey that will clarify and sharpen our truest gifts and identities.

I am reminded of perhaps the greatest sculptor the world has known, Michelangelo. His art form did not begin when he first picked up a hammer and chisel and struck stone. His art form began in a dusty quarry, judging the quality of great slabs of marble.

Young Michelangelo had to learn how to look at rough-hewn marble and envision what could be created from it. Once he had selected what he thought was a suitable piece of marble, he had to live with the stone for a while. After having the marble delivered to his studio, he would rise with the dawn each morning and examine it. He had learned from the great masters that the soft, slanting dawn light is best for catching a glimpse inside the translucent marble, for seeing the veins of the rock, the hidden flaws, the character that is unique to that one piece of marble. Only after spending time understanding the rock would Michelangelo begin to shape it with a chisel and hammer.

This is what Jesus was doing to Simon. In the early dawn of their friendship he was looking deep inside Simon's soul and seeing the character lines as well as the flaws that needed to be developed and shaped over time. But above all, this master sculptor of men and women was saying: "This is rock, very fine rock. He will make a fine disciple."

Again I think of my friend, the young man who nearly died at the rock concert. Today, thirty years later, he has earned a doctorate in theology and is a specialist in training minsters to be chaplains and counselors in hospitals and other healing institutions. When my friend was introduced to Jesus, Jesus looked deep into his fractured life and saw qualities that this young man never knew were there. The spirit of Christ slowly identified these qualities, carved his character out of rock, and is still in the process of creating a masterpiece.

When we are first introduced to Jesus, we cannot see ourselves as Jesus sees us. But he looks deep inside and knows us for who we are. He figuratively gives us a name known only to him. It is our special name. And he sets us on the pathway of becoming the name that is our own. For Peter it was "Rock." For you it may be mercy or justice or grace or hospitality or humor. But if you follow Jesus long enough—and willfully allow him to shape your life—he will carve from the depths of your rock the best qualities within you.

Reflections
Psalm 42:1-2, John 12:26

Guido the plumber and Michelangelo obtained their marble from the same quarry, but what each saw in the marble made the difference between a nobleman's sink and a brilliant sculpture.
    —*Bob Kall*[3]

A rock pile ceases to be a rock pile the moment a single man contemplates it, bearing within him the image of a cathedral.
    —*Antoine de Saint-Exupéry*[4]

In forming His group, on whom so much depended, Christ had to use ordinary people. The rock on which He built His church was the rubble of common human nature.

—*Elton Trueblood*[5]

Dear God,

More than anything I want to ask with Andrew, "Where are you staying?" I want to know how to reach you, how to talk with you, how to live in your presence. Slowly I have come to understand, Lord, that you do not dwell in a physical place. Rather you are in every place at once. You are beyond the limits of time and measurable space. Your true home is always in the realm of relationship. And I yearn to be in relationship with you.

Lord, as with Peter, you know me better than I know myself. You see in me traits I cannot discern. You yearn for me to actualize my God-breathed potential. Call forth my greatest gifts, O God. Carve the contours of my character from the rough-hewn stone of my life. I want to be God-shaped, chiseled in your image.

Lord, I do not know where you are leading me. But help me to accept your invitation: "Come, and you will see." Amen.

Questions among Friends

1. If you grew up in a Christian home, when did you begin the transition from Christianity being a family tradition to it being a personally chosen faith and commitment? Did a certain event or experience in your life cause you to explore Christianity and to desire to become a Christian?

2. If you did not grow up in a Christian home, what has caused you to want to explore and inquire about Christianity—to find out with Andrew *where God is staying?*

3. Who is the Andrew in your life, the one who is most responsible for introducing you to Jesus and the Christian faith?

4. Do you know someone whom you would like to introduce to Jesus?

5. Describe an event in your life that jolted you—like my friend at the rock concert—and caused you to think more deeply about your need to draw closer to God.

6. If you are in a discussion group, think of some nicknames, like "Rock," that Jesus might give to the friends sitting around you. What spiritual gifts and strengths do you perceive in your friends that Jesus might identify and develop?

Chapter Two

"COME, FOLLOW ME . . ."

Now after John had been taken into custody, Jesus came into Galilee, preaching the gospel of God, and saying, "The time is fulfilled, and the kingdom of God is at hand; repent and believe in the gospel."

As He was going along by the Sea of Galilee, He saw Simon and Andrew, the brother of Simon, casting a net in the sea; for they were fishermen. And Jesus said to them, "Follow Me, and I will make you become fishers of men." Immediately they left their nets and followed Him. Going on a little farther, He saw James the son of Zebedee, and John his brother, who were also in the boat mending the nets. Immediately He called them; and they left their father Zebedee in the boat with the hired servants, and went away to follow Him. (Mark 1:14-20 [Matthew 4:18-22, Luke 5:1-11])

JESUS BEGAN HIS MINISTRY IN THE MIDST OF INTENSE CRISIS AND danger. Soon after Jesus' baptism in the Jordan Valley, John the Baptist was arrested by Herod Antipas and thrown into prison. Herod was infuriated that John was preaching against his sexual immorality, and, in particular, deriding his sister-in-law, Herodias (Mark 6:17). Jesus immediately withdrew into the calmer northern environs of the Sea of Galilee. Suddenly it was not safe to be associated with John.

Arriving in Galilee, Jesus moved from Nazareth to live in Capernaum, which became the central hub for his ministry. Capernaum was also the home of five of the twelve disciples: Peter, Andrew, James, John, and Matthew (sometimes called Levi).

Since 1856, Capernaum has been identified with the present-day Tell Hum and is in the process of being excavated by archaeologists. The synagogue in which Jesus taught has been discovered and, very likely, so has Peter's house.[1]

In Jesus' day Capernaum was a thriving fishing village, and fishing was a lucrative business. Pork was forbidden by Jewish dietary law, and lamb was reserved for special occasions and festivities. Fish was therefore the staple source of protein for all of Palestine. Fish were caught in the Sea of Galilee, preserved by salting in towns such as Tarichae, and marketed throughout Israel.

Peter and Andrew were involved in a successful fishing partnership with James and John and their father, Zebedee (Luke 5:10). We do not know how affluent they were, but their partnership was large enough to comprise multiple boats and employ additional laborers (Mark 1:20, Luke 5:2). Though they were not rich, the men in this partnership probably made a good living.

In Capernaum Jesus began to teach and to heal, and it was in Capernaum that Jesus called his first disciples. Capernaum supplied pleasant days, close friends, and fond memories for Jesus. It was a place of good beginnings.

Discipleship Grows through Stages

My father was a pastor. When I was a small boy, I listened to him preach about Jesus first calling his disciples. In my young imagination, a vivid picture was etched. I could see Jesus—the bearded man in the striped robe, from my illustrated children's Bible—forcefully striding down a beach. He saw two total strangers who were mending their nets in a boat. Walking boldly up to them, he snared them with a hypnotic gaze and barked, "Come, follow me!" Captive to his command, they jumped out of their boat and scampered down the beach after this Pied Piper, never to return.

I was a seminary student before I realized that it didn't happen this way. Jesus did not approach strangers; he walked up to talk with some good friends. Introduced to Andrew and Peter through John the Baptist, Jesus had now lived in Capernaum for days. The Gospel of Mark suggests that Jesus stayed for a time in Peter's home. These men had eaten meals together and shared long conversations, and now these two brothers were watching the beginning days of Jesus' ministry.

Jesus would also have known James and John, the sons of Zebedee. Capernaum was not a large village. As Jesus grew in friendship with Andrew and Peter, he would have been introduced to the Zebedee family. They were probably a close clan.

We must understand that by the time Jesus asked these four fishing partners to "follow me" and be his disciples, they had already established a basis of friendship and familiarity with Jesus. There was a level of trust developing. Jesus was no stranger, and no mystical hypnotic stare was involved.

Jesus approaches most of us today in the same manner. He gradually and comfortably builds a relationship with us that slowly leads to greater involvement in ministry. In the case of Jesus' disciples, they grew through three distinct stages of discipleship.

First was a *friendship stage.* These fishermen had grown comfortable in Jesus' presence and realized that he was not a charlatan. The carpenter from Nazareth was trustworthy; they liked him and were attracted to him. And the feeling was mutual.

Second, they were formally asked to follow Jesus and moved into an *apprentice stage.* During Jesus' earthly ministry, they heard him teach, watched him heal, listened to him pray, witnessed his compassion, and saw his courage. It was from Jesus that they learned how to be ministers. Just as their fathers taught them how to fish for fish, Jesus now taught them how to fish for people.

Finally, following Jesus' resurrection, the disciples were thrust into a third stage, the *leadership stage.* If a Christian ministry and a Christian message were to follow Jesus' ascension, it was up to them. They were the leaders now. Enabled by the Holy Spirit, they had to be the presence of Jesus in the lives of those who were in need.

I suspect that if Jesus had walked up to Peter that day on the beach and said, "Peter, get out of your boat and come follow me to the Imperial City of Rome," Peter would have clamped his jaw, planted his feet, and stayed put. But thirty years later, when Peter did find himself giving leadership to the Christian community in Rome, his task felt natural. Slowly Peter had grown from friendship to apprenticeship to leadership.

When I first began to develop an adult friendship with Jesus, I was a college freshman, and much to my amazement, I was mesmerized by my first religion course. I enrolled in the course only because it was required to graduate from Furman University, a Baptist liberal arts university. The professor was a wonderful teacher and led me to explore thoughts I had never considered. Suddenly, I found I was interested in theology.

But I also experienced fear. Because my father was a pastor, I had an anxious dread that if I grew too close to Jesus, too involved in Christianity, I might be led to become a pastor as well, and that was the last thing this eighteen-year-old wanted to do.

Life is strange. Six years later when I was ordained a minister, it was the most natural thing in the world. Sure, I continued to balk at some of the "preacher stuff." I still do. But over time I had been slowly led from friendship to apprenticeship to leadership. It took six years. And the gradual spiritual growth fit me and felt comfortable.

All who would follow Jesus need to know that on our individual timetables, we will be asked to continue to grow and mature. And each of us, directed by our own spiritual gifts, will ultimately be led to the responsibility of leadership. Jesus calls every Christian to ministry. But he calls us each in our own way, in our own time, to our own task. As he would sometimes say to those first anxious disciples, "Take My yoke upon you, and learn from Me. . . . For My yoke is easy and My burden is light" (Matthew 11:29-30).

"Follow me . . ."

It is important to note that what Jesus asked of his would-be disciples required just two words: *follow me.* But hidden in those two words is the heart of understanding the process of Christian discipleship.

When Jesus called these simple fisherman, he did not ask them to adhere to a list of beliefs or sign a creed. He did not say, "Now, this is what I believe, and if you agree with me, I want you to follow me." He did not even say: "Before we begin, let's get straight about who I am. I may look like a carpenter and sound like a rabbi, but in truth I am God's promised Messiah. I am the Son of God." Jesus simply said "Follow me."

What Jesus was introducing is a method of learning truth. Some things can and some things cannot be learned from a book. Some things can be explained in a lecture or a conversation, and other things can be comprehended only through firsthand experience. Jesus was saying to his potential disciples: "There is only one way you can learn who I am and what I am about, and that is to follow me. Anything else that I might say to you today would be wasted breath."

Recently I spent several hours talking with an earnest young woman, Ann, about becoming a Christian. She is clearly interested, and she is incredibly bright. For the last few years Ann has been reading many books on religion: Zen Buddhism, Hinduism, eclectic New Age movements, and Christianity. Though stimulated and deepened by all her varied readings, she has slowly been drawn toward Christianity.

Above all, I learned that Ann is a person of remarkable integrity. And her integrity caused her to say to me: "Scott, I want to believe. I would like nothing better than to know that what the New Testament says is true. But it just can't be proven. I cannot know for sure that Jesus really did experience the resurrection. And if I can't become more sure of my beliefs, I don't see how I can claim to be a Christian."

I could relate to her perplexity because I have stood in her shoes. Finally I said: "Ann, if you have to have all the answers before making a commitment to be a Christian, you'll never be a Christian. The simple fact is that based on our best judgment and intuition—not ironclad proof—we step out on faith and begin to follow Jesus. Over time, through more than just intellect and reason, we become increasingly convinced that Christianity is true and that Jesus really is the Son of God."

This was true for Peter, Andrew, James, and John. It was only in walking with Jesus for three years—experiencing his teaching, his personality, his love, his spiritual depth, his death, and most of all, his resurrection—that they came to understand who Jesus was. Jesus could not explain this to them ahead of time; they had to experience life with Jesus for themselves.

One of my heroes is the recipient of the 1952 Nobel prize for peace, Dr. Albert Schweitzer. As a young man living in France and Germany, Schweitzer was one of the best known biblical scholars and theologians in the early years of the twentieth century. A man of great brilliance, Schweitzer was immersed in an intellectual climate in which the scientific method and human reason were thought to be able to unravel most mysteries and solve the world's greatest problems. Of course, the horrors of World War I quickly put a damper on such optimism.

In the midst of these heady days of reason and intellectual pursuit, Schweitzer set out on an academic quest to "discover the historical Jesus." In other words, using newfound methods of historical research and literary criticism, Schweitzer was confident that he could gain a much more precise picture of who Jesus was, what exactly he said, and how he should be understood. The culmination of his studies is found in a now classic book titled *The Quest of the Historical Jesus.*

I was required to read this book in seminary for a course in the history of New Testament criticism. It was not an easy tome to comprehend. However, as I labored through its musty pages, I could detect that by the end of Schweitzer's quest to intellectually remove the shroud of mystery from Jesus, his basic conclusion was that the mystery could not be penetrated, that the truth of Jesus could not be intellectually proven, that the credibility of the life and teachings of Jesus could never be reduced to courtroom proof and scientific validation.

Yet what impressed me most about this book was the last paragraph on the final page, when Schweitzer brings all that he has learned from his "quest" down to one statement. Reading this paragraph late one night, I realized that I was interacting with one of the most profound statements ever written by a Christian. Schweitzer writes of Jesus:

> He comes to us as one unknown, without a name, as of old, by the lakeside, he came to those men who did not know who he was. He says the same words: "Follow me!" and sets us to those tasks which he must fulfil in our time. He commands. And to those who hearken to him, whether wise or unwise, he will reveal himself in the peace, the labours, the conflicts and the suffering that they may experience in his fellowship, and as an ineffable mystery they will learn who he is.[2]

Schweitzer is absolutely right. You do not grasp certainty about the validity and credibility of Jesus and *then* begin to follow him. Rather, based on your best judgment, intellectual probability (not proof), and spiritual guidance, you step out on faith and say, "Okay, Jesus, I'm going to walk with you for awhile." And, as Schweitzer says, Jesus will reveal himself in our peace and work, conflicts and suffering, and we will learn who he is.

I'm happy to say that my friend Ann came to this same conclusion. Exhausted by primarily an intellectual approach to understanding Christianity, she finally said: "All right, I'll try it. I'll walk with Jesus for awhile and keep my eyes, heart, and mind open. We'll see." Now she is learning for herself who Jesus is.

Becoming a Christian does not begin by signing a creed, accepting certain fundamental truth propositions, or capturing Jesus in a test tube. Rather, it begins when, based on an emerging friendship with Jesus, we say, "Okay, I'll follow you for a time and see what happens." Jesus may not be who we think he is. He is always much more. And he never fails to reveal himself through the work, conflicts, and suffering we pass through in his fellowship. Jesus' way of teaching disciples is the "follow me" method.

And I Will Make You Become Fishers of Men

Jesus is clear that the result of following him is that you will become fishers of men and women. Using a nice turn of phrase, Jesus is saying that the purpose of Christianity is to help other people.

Christianity has always maintained a strong focus on the spiritual disciplines. Healthy and growing Christians must participate in meditation, prayer, and the devotional life. We believe in cultivating an inner life that results in personal spiritual health. But for the Christian, a major purpose of strengthening the inner spiritual life is to enable us to reach out and help others in the name of Jesus.

Jesus intentionally taught his disciples to pray. He emphasized the power and the necessity of prayer. But the purpose of Jesus' prayer life was to draw spiritual strength and direction from his Father so he could in turn meet the spiritual and physical needs of those around him.

After writing *The Quest of the Historical Jesus,* Albert Schweitzer came to a major turning point in his life. At the time he was not only an internationally known biblical scholar, but also a widely acclaimed authority on the music of Johann Sebastian Bach and a popular concert organist. But as Schweitzer neared midlife, he was not satisfied by his own accolades. He was haunted by his deepening awareness of human suffering in the world. Though he could have stayed in the ivory towers and concert halls of Europe, he grew increasingly uncomfortable. He found that he could not immerse himself in the life and teachings of Jesus in an academic world and turn his back on human need.

Finally he decided to go to medical school. After he graduated, he left Europe, at the age of thirty-eight, to go to French Equatorial Africa (now Gabon) to build a hospital in a remote jungle area where medical care was inaccessible. For the rest of his life, Schweitzer became a fisher of people, casting a broad net of love and care to those who could not help themselves. His ability to live like Jesus resulted in many Africans deciding to follow Jesus.

To follow Jesus is ultimately to learn that we are not placed on this earth to live for ourselves—we are created to live for others. Despite our varied vocations, every Christian has the same purpose in life: we are to be fishers of men and women. And the net that we use is made of the strong fabric of God's love.

Taking a Chance

In one sense, when Peter, Andrew, James, and John left their boats to follow Jesus, little changed. They did not sell their boats and fold their fishing partnership. Indeed, three years later, immediately following the death of Jesus, we find these four men back at the Sea of Galilee fishing as before.

Yet there came a time when these young fishing partners looked back and realized that the day when Jesus said, "Come, follow me!" changed everything. It was the major turning point in their life. It was the day they decided to take a risk and follow Jesus.

As Christians, we have moments when we must take a chance and walk into the unknown, following Jesus. Søren Kierkegaard was a brilliant, young Danish philosopher who lived in the nineteenth century. His bright intellect was both a blessing and a curse. As he studied Christianity, he could provide cogent arguments both for and against the Christian faith. Attracted to Christianity and yet racked by doubt, Kierkegaard often reflected on the words of the French mathematician-philosopher Blaise Pascal, who in the dark night of his own soul cried out, "Seeing too much to deny and too little to be sure, I am in a state to be pitied."[3] Yet Kierkegaard ultimately came to see that intellect could take him only so far. At some point he knew he must stand on a precipice and take what he called a great "leap of faith."

Kierkegaard took the leap. Months later he looked back to that decisive moment, and wrote in his journal, "During the first period of a man's life the greatest danger is: not to take the risk."[4]

For everyone who becomes a Christian, there comes that moment of leaving one's nets, of taking the leap, of letting go. The future beckons, and we decide to take the chance. We follow Jesus.

Years ago, as a twenty-three-year-old, I sat on a stone wall late one autumn night in North Carolina and pondered my unsure future. Like Kierkegaard and Pascal, I too had seen too much about Christianity to doubt and too little to be sure. Yet I had to decide if Christianity would direct my future, or if I would walk away from that wall "the master of my fate, the captain of my soul."

That afternoon I had been reading a book by the philosopher Elton Trueblood titled *A Place to Stand.* Trueblood snared my attention when I read:

> At the deepest points of his life it is required of a man that he be a gambler, and in our greatest gamble it is reasonable to allow the testimony of Christ to tip the balance. A Christian is one who bets his life that Christ is right.[5]

I had never before been a betting man. But in the quietness of that night, I realized that the success of my life depended on taking reasonable chances. I slowly slid down off the wall and awkwardly began to follow Jesus. Now, twenty-seven years later, I realize that was the most fate-hinged moment of my life. It was the moment from which I tell time: before and after. It was the moment when Jesus walked down the shoreline of my life, and I heard an old friend say, "Come, follow me."

Reflections
Mark 9:22-24, John 12:25-26

It has been said that a modern man is one who is able to understand but unable to act decisively.
—*Anonymous*

We understand more than we know.
—*Blaise Pascal*[6]

Nothing will ever be attempted, if all possible objections must be first overcome.
—*Dr. Samuel Johnson*[7]

Woe to the man whose heart has not learned while young to hope, to love, to put his trust in life.
—*Joseph Conrad*[8]

Dear Father,

I yearn to know more than I am capable of understanding. I want to glimpse my destination before I make the journey. I long to fathom the mystery of Jesus without walking with him for years. I anxiously seek sure answers in a life that demands risk and chance and blind courage.

May I listen to the quiet, simple voice of Jesus who says, "Follow me!" and trust that your Spirit will show me the way. Give me the ability to leave my boat, abandon my nets, and become a fisher of men and women. Amen.

Questions among Friends

1. In which stage of discipleship do you see yourself: friendship, apprenticeship, or leadership?

2. As you follow Jesus in the present chapter of your life, what is he teaching you? What learning issue are you facing or experiencing?

3. What labors, conflicts, and sufferings in your past have taught you the most about Jesus and the Christian faith?

4. What issues make it most difficult for you to follow Jesus or to accept the Christian faith? What causes you to intellectually doubt?

5. Can you describe a specific moment or memory when you realized that the Spirit of Jesus was saying to you, "Come, follow me!" and you "took the risk" and responded?

6. How is God's Spirit presently leading you to become a fisher of people? What opportunity do you have to help someone else who is in physical or spiritual need? Is there a specific person whom you are trying to introduce to Jesus?

John 12:25+26

Chapter Three

THE STORMS OF LIFE

❧

And on that day, when evening came, He said to them, "Let us go over to the other side." Leaving the crowd, they took Him along with them in the boat, just as He was; and other boats were with Him. And there arose a fierce gale of wind, and the waves were breaking over the boat so much that the boat was already filling up. Jesus himself was in the stern, asleep on the cushion; and they woke Him and said to Him, "Teacher, do You not care that we are perishing?" And he got up and rebuked the wind and said to the sea, "Hush, be still." And the wind died down and it became perfectly calm. And He said to them, "Why are you afraid? How is it that you have no faith?" They became very much afraid and said to one another, "Who then is this, that even the wind and the sea obey Him?" (Mark 4:35-41 [Matthew 8:23-27, Luke 8:22-25])

WE EACH HAVE CRITICAL TIMES IN OUR LIVES WHEN GRAVE PROBLEMS overwhelm us and we feel like we are drowning and going under for the final time. We are terrified and lose confidence that things will ever be better. Panic threatens to overcome our reason and stifle our faith.

As John Mark listened to Roman Christians caught in the anguish of Nero's cruel persecution, he knew that many of his brothers and sisters were paralyzed by fear. He decided to relate to them a story about a time when Jesus and his disciples faced the horror of a fierce storm at sea that nearly destroyed them.

As the story begins, much had happened around the small village of Capernaum since Jesus had asked Peter, Andrew, James, and John to "follow me." First, Jesus had been publicly recognized as a powerful and gifted healer. He had cast out a demon from a man, under the roof of the local synagogue. Most important to Peter, Jesus had entered Peter's home and cured his mother-in-law of an illness (Mark 1:29-31). Later, he healed a man of leprosy, enabled a paralytic to walk, and made a man's withered hand healthy. People were awestruck by the healing power of God that was emanating through Jesus. As a result, crowds began to gather around him, and the sick lined up to be healed.[1]

Second, Jesus was being recognized as a persuasive and controversial teacher. But more than being wise, learned, or eloquent, what impressed people—and infuriated others—was the absolute authority with which he spoke (Mark 1:22). He talked not as a rabbi who wanted to explain the meaning of the scriptures, but rather as if he had direct authority and power from God. For instance, after he caused a paralytic to walk, he exclaimed to the man, "Son, your sins are forgiven." This shocked some of the scribes who were watching, and they exclaimed: "Why does this man speak that way? He is blaspheming; who can forgive sins but God alone?" (Mark 2:5-7).

The result was that early in his ministry, Jesus clashed with Jewish religious authorities. As Mark 3:6 relates, "The Pharisees went out and immediately began conspiring with the Herodians against Him, as to how they might destroy Him." Jesus knew that John the Baptist had overstepped his bounds and was now in Herod's dungeon facing execution. Jesus was aware that he was tempting the same fate.

Jesus' family in Nazareth also realized the danger confronting Jesus. Mark alone has the boldness to record in his Gospel that Jesus' family thought that he had "lost his senses," and they came to "take custody of him" (Mark 3:20-21). Even Jesus' family thought that Jesus had gone too far; that he was perhaps emotionally unstable; that he needed to be rescued and brought home while there was still time.

Mark is clear. Within a period of a few months after beginning his public ministry in Capernaum, Jesus was seen by his disciples, the crowds, the scribes and Pharisees, and even his own family as being radically different. You liked him or you hated him. But either way you paid attention to him. Such attention provoked danger.

The third event that occurred early in Jesus' ministry was that he officially called twelve men to be his disciples, so that "they would be with Him and that He could send them out to preach" (Mark 3:13-19). Jesus was moving beyond the friendship stage. He was formally saying to twelve men: "I want you to be my disciples. I want you to grow from being just good friends to being my apprentices."

In the midst of gathering storm clouds with the Jewish authorities, Jesus and his fledgling disciples are confronted with a physical storm on the Sea of Galilee. The storm becomes the setting for profound lessons concerning Christian discipleship.

Forced to Ask the Right Questions

The Sea of Galilee is not a sea at all but a natural lake, formed by the Jordan River flowing down from the north, bearing water from as far away as Mount Hermon. Ten miles north of the Sea of Galilee, the Jordan creates the small, marshy Lake Huleh, which is 230 feet above sea level. However, when the Jordan flows out of the lower end of Lake Huleh and moves south again toward the Sea of Galilee, the water cascades from 230 feet *above* sea level to 685 feet *below* sea level in less than ten miles.

Surrounded by mountains, the Sea of Galilee is seven miles wide and thirteen miles long. It is a deep lake, dropping off quickly from the shoreline and reaching depths of 150 feet. It is the sudden depth of the lake that enables violent storms to produce towering waves.

On the day that the disciples experienced the harrowing storm, Jesus had been teaching to a large crowd. So dense and pressing was the crowd that Jesus was speaking from the bow of a boat moored off the shore, where people could not physically reach him. As evening approached, rather than beach the boat near the crowd, the disciples sailed with Jesus directly to the other side of the lake.

As the sky darkened, the wind began to roar down a natural wind tunnel formed by the steep rift valley and lash across the placid lake. Quickly kicking up white caps, the wind turned the flat surface of the lake into high, terrifying waves.

Squalls were nothing new to veteran fishermen such as Peter. They understood Galilean storms and their intensity. But this was evidently not your normal storm—and these fishermen knew this. Soon the situation was out of control, and the boat began to swamp. If the ship sank in darkness in this violent sea, they were doomed.

Jesus was exhausted. He lay in a deep sleep in the stern with his head leaning on the wood and leather kneeling pad normally used by the helmsman. Incredulous at his ability to sleep in the midst of the storm, the desperate disciples finally woke him. Staring into the fury of the storm, Jesus shouted commanding words into the face of the wind, words that literally mean "be muzzled" or "be gagged." From that moment the storm began to abate, until it became calm in the blackness of the night. In the midst of the darkness, Jesus turned and confronted the disciples with words these rugged men never forgot: "Why are you afraid? How is it that you have no faith?"

Perhaps the silence in the boat was deafening as twelve tired, exhausted, and chastened men went limp with relief. But somewhere there was whispering. And the murmuring voices were saying, "Who then is this, that even the wind and the sea obey Him?"

The primary theme of this story is that the disciples gained insight into Jesus in a way that could never be taught by words or illustration during a calm day on dry land. Granted, they did not gain a lot of answers. But at least they formed the right question: "Who then is this?" And the right questions are always better than the wrong answers.

For these novice disciples, it was one thing to marvel at a miracle of healing. That was something that happened to somebody else. But to have your own life thrown into jeopardy, to be reduced to quivering fear and terror, to believe that your life is over, and then to have Jesus calm the storm—well, that's another matter. Such moments of radical insecurity broke the disciples loose from their normal state of mind and allowed new and impenetrable truth to begin to filter through at a profound feeling level.

For all disciples of Jesus, it is the storms of life that provide our real learning experiences. We simply cannot learn without pain and anxiety. Almost every spiritual truth that I cling to has come out of the cauldron and kiln of my own difficult moments.

One of my favorite books is the late Henri Nouwen's *The Wounded Healer*. His theme is that most of us can trace our gifts for ministry directly to our own experiences of recovering from the major wounds in our life. Perhaps the greatest tragedy in my life was the sudden death of my father when I was fourteen, a wound that has never fully healed. Yet it has been the experience of going through this storm that has taught me the most about God, theology, my self, and how to minister to others. My woundedness has enabled me to be a healer.

Again, remember the words of Albert Schweitzer, "He will reveal himself in the peace, the labours, the conflicts, and the suffering that they may experience in his fellowship." In the company of Jesus, the disciples survived a storm. And the storm shook their theology loose. The storm ravaged their souls and blew away preconceived notions. It made them discard wrong answers and ask the right question, "Who then is this?"

Without storms we never get a first-rate education. And without storms we are not worth our salt as disciples of Jesus.

Teacher, Do You Not Care That We Are Perishing?

Mark's choice to place this story of the storm in his Gospel was made with great intent and deliberation. For if anything was true about the Christians to whom he was writing in Rome, it was that they were going through one horrendous storm. In the midst of the persecution ordered by the Roman emperor, Nero, most of them felt that all was lost, and they were asking searching questions: "Where is God in the midst of our pain and crisis? Why doesn't God stop this torment? Why are innocent Christians burned as torches and torn apart by wild animals? Does God not care? How much longer can we stand this pain?"

To these questions the story of the stilling of the storm makes this reply: *Christians are not protected from the storms of life. But we can be assured that with God's help, they will not destroy us.*

First, let's look at the statement, "Christians are not protected from the storms of life." It is a simple fact that to become a Christian does not mean that you get a better life insurance rating. In fact, more Christians were martyred for their faith in the twentieth century than in any century since the life of Jesus. It can be a dangerous thing to be a Christian.

To become a Christian also does not mean that you become immune to cancer, are spared car wrecks, or have a better chance than others to avoid personal tragedy. And though having the peace of Christ in our heart can lead to better physical, spiritual, and emotional health, Christians still experience their full share of loss and tragedy.

However, the real point that John Mark is wanting Christians in Rome to understand is that when Jesus is with you in the midst of the storm, you will not be destroyed. I saw this truth revealed in the lives of two of my friends.

J. D. and Carolyn Hudson are deeply devoted Christians. Their close and intimate marriage had lasted nearly fifty years. Several years ago, however, Carolyn discovered that she had breast cancer. During the course of months, she endured surgery, chemotherapy, radiation, and every form of experimental drug that might be helpful. Yet the cancer continued to spread and to ravage her body.

J. D. is a Texas rancher and retired bank president. He is also as tough as a boot. As a Navy veteran of World War II, he has seen his share of storms. But J. D. had never seen his wife suffer. To pray fervently day after day for healing, and yet see Carolyn continue to decline, was almost more than J. D. could bear. He naturally began to ask with the Christians in Rome: "Where are you, God? When will you answer our prayers? Why won't you rescue us from this suffering?"

Over the months it became increasingly obvious that Carolyn could not be medically healed from her cancer. The issue became not only a question of healing but a question of "Is this storm going to destroy our family? Is this storm going to blow away our faith and drown our souls in despondency?"

One day Carolyn called me and asked me to come by her house for a conversation. As I sat alone with Carolyn in her living room, she looked dreadfully weak. But pulling herself together, she said: "Scott, I know I am dying, and I will not live much longer. But, Scott, we've all got to die sometime. That's life. But thank God, I've had a wonderful life. And today I want to talk with you about my funeral. I don't want J. D. to have to worry about planning my funeral when I'm gone. Let's just give God thanks for life, and face death together."

As I left her home, I realized that Carolyn was a woman who was not being destroyed by the greatest storm she had ever faced. Waves might be towering over her, but she was as calm as Jesus. She did not want to die. But she realized that death was inevitable. Her faith in the goodness of God was keeping the storm at bay, her ship afloat.

A few weeks later, Carolyn entered the hospital for the final time. On the morning she died, J. D. stood by her bed surrounded by his two adult sons and several of his closest friends. J. D. realized he was not in the boat alone. Others were riding through the storm with him. Though he was emotionally frazzled and grief stricken, his faith in God was strong. He knew that somehow this terrible storm would not destroy him or his family.

The time came when Carolyn's body surrendered to disease and her soul began to move toward eternity. Lying in a comatose state and barely breathing, Carolyn's eyes suddenly fluttered, and those closest to her could clearly hear her say, "I'm crossing over. . . . The door is open. . . . I'm crossing over." She breathed her last breath with words of faith and hope on her lips.

Since Carolyn's death, J. D. and I occasionally meet for breakfast just to check up on each other. I can tell you that though the death of Carolyn broke his heart, it did not destroy this good, Christian man. And though he would not choose to endure such a fierce storm again, he will tell you that he is learning things from that tempest that he could learn in no other way. Above all, he has discovered that tragedies we think we cannot endure can indeed be weathered if Jesus Christ is with us.

After enduring much suffering and turmoil in his own life, the Apostle Paul wrote these profound words to Christians in Rome:

> In the same way the Spirit also helps our weakness; for we do not know how to pray as we should, but the Spirit Himself intercedes for us with groanings too deep for words; . . .
>
> And we know that God causes all things to work together for good to those who love God, to those who are called according to His purpose. . . .
>
> What then shall we say to these things? If God is for us, who is against us? He who did not spare His own Son, but delivered Him over for us all, how will He not also with Him freely give us all things? . . . For I am convinced that neither death, nor life, nor angels, nor principalities, nor things present, nor things to come, nor powers, nor height, nor depth, nor any other created thing, will be able to separate us from the love of God, which is in Christ Jesus our Lord. (Romans 8:26-39)

What Paul was able to see is that God went through the same agony when his son, Jesus, was arrested, tortured, and gruesomely crucified. As Paul perceived, God "did not spare His own son." God did not lift the rules of natural law and invade history to spare Jesus, any more than he spared the Christians in Rome their suffering under Nero. History is history. Natural law is natural law. People are born and people die. Life itself can be hell. And Jesus caught his share of hell.

But God did not leave things there. Through the resurrection of Jesus, we are able to perceive much more to life than we can see, that beyond death is life. And that "God causes all things to work together for good to those who love God, to those who are called according to His purpose."

A Word about Miracles

As a young theology student, I was disturbed about the whole issue of miracles in the New Testament. I am by nature a hard-nosed realist. I don't believe that God is about the business of overriding natural law so that I can be "miraculously" cured from cancer—while someone else dies. I am not saying that faith and prayer cannot have great and positive effects on our ability to grow healthier. Even modern science is finding this to be true. But God does not alter the laws of nature for my convenience or for yours. When I fall down the steps, gravity is not suspended.

So how do we deal with the miracle stories of Jesus? Did Jesus perform miracles or did he not? I believe that he did.

Why do I believe this? For me, it all boils down to the issue of the resurrection of Jesus. Paul states the issue clearly, "If Christ has not been raised, then our preaching is vain, your faith also is vain" (1 Corinthians 15:14). If the power of God did not raise Jesus from the dead—the greatest miracle of all—then Christianity is one of the greatest hoaxes perpetrated on the human race. If there was no resurrection, then Jesus was only a profound teacher, a powerful prophet, a loving man, but certainly not the Son of God. And our faith is in vain.

After much study I came as a young adult to affirm the intellectual credibility of the resurrection of Jesus. Yet I often wanted to affirm the resurrection and discount the miracles, or at least make them scientifically understandable. One day I realized the great inconsistency in my thought.

If I was willing to affirm that God could do the miraculous in the life of Jesus through the resurrection, why did I then deny the fact that God could do the miraculous through Jesus' life and ministry as well? I finally came to affirm that in this one man—Jesus of Nazareth, the Son of God—God the Father worked in a *unique way* to reveal himself. In a specific window of time and through a specific individual, God used miracles to teach us of his love, compassion, power, and support of our lives.

Now, I admit that I do not fully understand the paradox of miracles today, and I can't explain miracles in the life of Jesus. They mystify me and frustrate my logical mind, as they did the first disciples. But this one thing I know to be true: If I affirm the historical truth of the resurrection—and I do—then it is inconsistent to believe that the same power of God that raised Jesus from the dead was not also available through Jesus for healing and the stilling of storms.

As Christian disciples, we will all experience our fair share of storms. They will scare us to death. But through the trials and tragedies of life, we will learn that God's sustaining Spirit is with us in the midst of all events. And when the Spirit of God protects us, we will not be destroyed.

Reflections
Psalm 46:1-4,10; Proverbs 29:25; 2 Thessalonians 3:3; 1 Peter 3:13

God moves in a mysterious way
His wonders to perform;
He plants his footstep in the sea,
And rides upon the storm.
   —William Cowper[2]

God is good, there is no devil but fear.
   —Elbert Hubbard[3]

As sure as God puts his children in the furnace he will be in the furnace with them.
   —Charles H. Spurgeon[4]

The miracles are a retelling in small letters of the very same story which is written across the whole world in letters too large for some of us to see.
   —C. S. Lewis[5]

There is no spiritual life without persistent struggle and interior conflict.
   —Thomas Merton[6]

Tell me, I'll forget.
Show me, I may remember.
But involve me and I'll understand.
    —*Ancient Chinese Proverb*

Dear Father,

Only through storm can I learn of you. Give me the courage to accept that fear is the dark side of faith, that there is no peace without conflict. May I take comfort in knowing that you are a God who "plants his footstep in the sea, and rides upon the storm." Amen.

Questions among Friends

1. Describe a *storm* you have encountered in your life that has taught you much about your relationship with God and the Christian faith. What was one lesson that you learned through experiencing this storm?

2. Do you sometimes struggle with the aspect of miracles in the New Testament? How have you resolved this issue in your own thinking? Do you believe that a miracle is the result of God *suspending* the effect of natural law or God *using* natural law in a way that we have not yet come to understand?

3. What have you learned from reflecting on the disciple's encounter with the storm at sea? How does this ancient story apply to your own life today?

4. Reflect for a moment on the ancient Chinese proverb: "Tell me, I'll forget. Show me, I may remember. But involve me and I'll understand." How is God *involving* you in life so that you will better understand the nature of God and the truth of Christianity?

Chapter Four

WALKING ON THE WATER

Immediately Jesus made His disciples get into the boat and go ahead of Him to the other side to Bethsaida, while He Himself was sending the crowd away. After bidding them farewell, He left for the mountain to pray.

When it was evening, the boat was in the middle of the sea, and He was alone on the land. Seeing them straining at the oars, for the wind was against them, at about the fourth watch of the night He came to them, walking on the sea; and He intended to pass by them. But when they saw Him walking on the sea, they supposed that it was a ghost, and cried out; for they all saw Him and were terrified. But immediately He spoke with them and said to them, "Take courage; it is I, do not be afraid." Then He got into the boat with them, and the wind stopped; and they were utterly astonished, for they had not gained any insight from the incident of the loaves, but their heart was hardened. (Mark 6:45-52 [Matthew 14:22-33, John 6:16-21])

Peter said to [Jesus], "Lord, if it is You, command me to come to You on the water. And He said, "Come!" And Peter got out of the boat, and walked on the water and came toward Jesus. But seeing the wind, he became frightened, and beginning to sink, he cried out, "Lord, save me!" Immediately Jesus stretched out His hand and took hold of him, and said to him, "You of little faith, why did you doubt?" (Matthew 14:28-31)

THE DANGER CONFRONTING JESUS WAS ESCALATING. THE PHARISEES were openly orchestrating a campaign against him. His unorthodox attitude toward the Jewish law infuriated them. As crowds grew increasingly larger wherever Jesus appeared, it was impossible for him to move quietly and inconspicuously. Trouble brewed.

Events spiraled to crisis proportions one day on a lonely lakeshore. Jesus had just fed a crowd of five thousand hungry and impoverished peasants by miraculously multiplying five small loaves of bread and two salted fish. Only the Gospel of John gives clear insight into the nature of the crisis. John writes, "Jesus, perceiving that they were intending to come and take Him by force to make Him king, withdrew again to the mountain by Himself alone" (John 6:15). An excited crowd, now convinced that Jesus was Messiah, was eager to place him on their shoulders and march off to Jerusalem. Any person who could feed five thousand people from a small boy's lunch was certainly capable of calling down catastrophe from heaven upon the Roman legions. If Moses could deliver the Hebrew children from Pharaoh, certainly Jesus could now deliver their descendants from Caesar.

Jesus was aware of the danger he would face if word filtered back to the Romans that yet another political uprising was brooding in Galilee. For a moment, consider a tragic event that Jesus had personally witnessed in his short lifetime.

Jesus was raised in Nazareth, a small, mountainous village located three miles northwest of Sepphoris, the administrative capital of southern Galilee. Sepphoris, not Nazareth, was likely the center of Jesus' cultural, political, and economic world.

In A.D. 6, when Jesus was around ten years old, a violent event transpired in Sepphoris, one which Jesus could not have forgotten. Judas the Galilean staged a tax revolt and raided the royal arsenal in Sepphoris. Varus, the Roman governor of Syria, retaliated with an iron fist. Marching from Antioch, Varus's troops burned Sepphoris to the ground. Then, chasing the fleeing rebels into the countryside, Varus rounded up the ringleaders and crucified two thousand men in public places. The stench of bloated, rotten corpses hanging on hastily made crosses fouled the air near Nazareth for weeks.[1]

Herod Antipas, the son of Herod the Great, immediately began to rebuild the charred city of Sepphoris. Much of the carpentry work that Joseph and Jesus obtained in future years was probably related to this massive reconstruction process. With hammer and saw in hand, Jesus had many occasions to reflect on the severity of Roman justice and how violently Roman governors would react to the disturbance of the peace. Jesus knew what happened to Jews who led political movements.

Now, years later, Jesus faced the ecstatic crowd whom he had fed. They were wide-eyed and frothing at the mouth, eager to stage one more rebellion, to declare that he should be king of Israel. Jesus knew that if he did not disperse this crowd and silence their clamoring, he would be executed by Rome long before he could fulfill his ministry.

Both Mark and Matthew report that Jesus calmed the crowd in this manner: "Immediately Jesus made His disciples get into the boat and go ahead of Him to the other side to Bethsaida, while he Himself was sending the crowd away." Why did Jesus first send the disciples away before he attempted to calm the crowd?

Many New Testament scholars are of the opinion that at this stage in Jesus' ministry, his disciples were sympathetic to the emotions of the crowd. They too saw Jesus' future—and their future—cast in the cultural expectations of their day. If Jesus was to be Messiah, then he must be a political king, a mighty warrior, a leader of the Jewish nation. Only after the resurrection would they begin to understand what the term "Son of God" really meant. Along with the crowds, the disciples wanted Jesus to speed up the process, to rally the Galilean populace around him and move on to Jerusalem.[2]

If indeed this was the situation, Jesus needed to separate his misguided disciples from the frenzied crowd. Jesus therefore "immediately . . . made His disciples get into the boat," and he sent them to the opposite side of the Sea of Galilee. Then Jesus firmly asked the crowd to go to their homes while he retreated to the sanctuary of the hills surrounding the lake. Jesus desperately needed to think, to ponder his future, and to pray for insight and guidance. It is against the backdrop of this tense moment that the disciples sailed into deepening dusk, to encounter Jesus walking on the water a few hours later.

Going Two Ways at Once

It was much easier and faster to sail directly across the Sea of Galilee than to travel by land around its shoreline. However, on this particular night, as the disciples sailed four-and-a-half miles east toward Bethsaida, the wind was blowing west, directly into their faces. In the midst of the dark night, the sail was probably dropped and oars distributed. Now, in the deep silence following midnight, all that could be heard was the howling wind, the creaking oars, and the labored breath and groans of tired men.

Sometime after three o'clock in the morning, perhaps as a setting moon filtered light through a cloud-mottled sky, someone became aware of another presence near them; not another boat, but a singular physical presence shrouded in darkness. Instantly the hair on the back of strong men's necks rose up, and an eerie fear seized them. The Jews believed that the spirits of the dead roamed large, wide-open regions such as deserts and oceans, and the folklore of Galilean fishermen was filled with stories of ghosts and apparitions. Brave men grew slack-jawed, and curses filled the air. Terror seized them. Then someone realized that it was not a ghost at all. It was Jesus.

Matthew alone relates to us that when Peter saw Jesus walking on the water, he was stupified. With muddled mind he blurted, "Lord, if it is You, command me to come to You on the water." Jesus told him to step out of the boat. Perhaps the greatest miracle of the night is that Peter actually did what he was told!

For a few tentative steps, all went well. Peter too walked on the surface of the water. Then he began to sink, screaming, "Lord, save me!" Jesus grabbed him, held him up, and gibed: "You of little faith, why did you doubt?"

It is interesting that the Greek word used by Matthew for doubt—*distazo*—is found in the Bible only in the Gospel of Matthew and only in this verse. It is a unique term, and literally means *to attempt to go in two directions at once.* This simple Greek word offers great insight into the dynamics of doubt.[3]

Peter's failure to stay on the surface of the water was not caused by a lack of courage or an absence of faith. He alone had the boldness to speak to the ghostly apparition before him. And he was the only disciple who dared to get out of the boat and attempt to do something that his experience and reason told him was impossible. Peter's problem occurred when he tried to go in two directions at once: to advance toward Jesus and simultaneously to retreat to the boat.

Perhaps this dynamic of *distazo*—of doubt—has been at the root of most of the problems in my life. I am not by nature a fearful or anxious person. A certain bold and quixotic character in me wants to pick up a lance and charge off on a stallion to take on the world. But I must admit that mixed in with my adventurous personality is also the trait of worry.

My oldest son, Drew, was home from college recently. Late one night I happened to overhear a conversation between Drew and his eighteen-year-old brother, Luke. Drew was laughing, and he said: "Luke, you know how Dad is. Everything can be perfectly all right, but he is going to find something to worry about!"

Though I was a little stung by those words, I couldn't help but grin and chuckle. Drew was right on target. He knows me well. The element of *distazo* is alive in the essence of my being. I am bold and fearful at once.

One of my favorite posters is a photograph of a young raccoon attempting to steal some fish left on a stringer inside a small fishing boat. The boat was loosely tied to a low dock. The inexperienced raccoon had come ambling down the dock, following the smell of pungent catfish baking in the sun. Spotting the fish in the bow of the boat, the raccoon decided to climb aboard for lunch. Gingerly placing his left front paw and left rear paw on the gunwale of the boat, he retained a firm grip on the dock with his right front paw and right rear paw. Suddenly the impact of his weight pushed the light boat away from the dock. The camera's shutter snapped at the exact instant that the raccoon found himself completely outstretched between boat and dock, and a split second away from plunging into the water. The raccoon was learning the difficult lesson that you can't hold on to the dock and climb into the boat at the same time.

Peter was learning the same lesson. You can't place your hands on the gunwale of Christian discipleship and hold on to the security of the world.

You can't keep your gaze on the encouraging face of Jesus if you are staring petrified at frothing waves. You simply cannot go two ways at once. Perhaps Jesus said it best: "No one can serve two masters; for either he will hate the one and love the other, or he will be devoted to one and despise the other. You cannot serve God and wealth" (Matthew 6:24).

One of the hardest lessons of Christian discipleship is to grasp the fact that God can be trusted; that if you step out of the security of your boat, you are not going to drown. You may sink a few hundred times before you finally learn that God is not going to let go of you. But God will never fail you. His arms are always there to pick you up and give you another chance.

Peter, a simple fisherman, learned that doubt is not primarily a matter of intellectual struggle. Rather, doubt is first and foremost the attempt to go in two directions at once: to trust the security of God and to fear the world simultaneously. Christians must slowly train themselves to focus only on the sustaining goodness of God.

The Courage to Fail

When Peter slipped beneath the waves, he was not sinking into an ignoble memory. Rather, he was cresting to one of the highest moments of his life. I believe that in the darkness of that night, Jesus had a smile on his face as he reached down to save Peter's life. At last one of his disciples had laid it on the line and risked failure. At least one of the twelve had crawled out of the boat of security and attempted to do something that only God could support and make happen. This was not a baby step into the water. It was a giant leap of faith.

To underscore a major theme in this book, *Christian disciples often learn best through failure.* And when we fail while attempting great things for God—even when doubt and fear cause our failure—we are winning a major victory in the eyes of God.

The famous country-western comedian Minnie Pearl suffered throughout childhood with a bad case of stage fright. Piano recitals were her particular bane. One day as she held on to her mother's skirt, refusing to walk out on the stage and play her recital piece, her mother took her by the arms, looked at her intently, and firmly said, "I want you to march right out there, young lady, and show them you can't play the piano!" It was a turning point in Minnie's life. Knowing that she had the freedom to fail, she sat down and played beautifully. Never again held captive by fear, she grew up to be a smashing entertainment success.

Too many Christian disciples are fixated in their growth process because they are afraid to fail. The truth is that some of the most profound failures have become the greatest saints. I think of St. Augustine of Hippo. For years he rambled around trying to find himself, dabbling with every philosophy or exotic teaching that came his way. In the process he lived with a young mistress and became the father of a son. Then he became a Christian. He could have looked at himself and said, "I'm a moral failure." He could have heard the old tapes that repeatedly played the message: "You'll never succeed. You always start out with a blaze of glory and slowly fade away." But Augustine did not allow himself to look in two directions at once, to be crushed by the waves of doubt. Instead he gave himself the freedom to fail and began to live a Christian life. He sank beneath the waves many times. But slowly he learned to walk on the waters of faith. Ultimately his many failures merged to form one incredible man used by the hands of God.

Disciples of Jesus are not people who always have their act together. Rather, Christians are people who fail, and fail a lot. The most mature have come to know that the only way to be formed into the image of Jesus is through the school of hard knocks. If you must know how to swim before you jump in the water, you'll never swim. And if you have to know how to walk on the water of faith before you climb out of your boat, you'll never follow Jesus. You must acknowledge the freedom to fail in order to have the ability to succeed.

Nearly thirty years ago, my aging New Testament professor, Dr. Frank Stagg, was commenting on Peter sinking beneath the waves. With balding pate and a fringe of hoary hair, Dr. Stagg suddenly looked up from his lecture notes and seized our class with his eagle's eyes. Conjuring up the wisdom of his years, he slowly expounded these words: "You need to know that Matthew does not intend to teach that failure does not matter, but that Christ does not fail even those who fail him." Those are words worth remembering.

Reflections

Psalm 37:5, Proverbs 3:5-6, Isaiah 26:3, Mark 9:23-24, Hebrews 10:23, James 1:5-7

We cannot live without support, but we must always be letting go of our support under pain of being left behind by the current of life, holding back instead of thrusting forward to grasp a new support. And always, in between, there is a zone of anxiety to be crossed. . . . What then is the force that holds men back, which prevents them from letting go of what they would like to let go? It is the middle-of-the-way anxiety.
   —Paul Tournier[4]

[Standing by the bed of her dying father, Judith Viorst wrote these words.]
You have grown wings of pain and flap around the bed like a wounded gull
calling for water, calling for tea, for grapes whose skins you cannot penetrate.
Remember when you taught me how to swim? Let go, you said, the lake will
hold you up. I long to say, Father, let go and death will hold you up.
   —*Judith Viorst*[5]

True religion should not say to us, "Obey! Conform! Reproduce the past!" It
should call upon us to grow, to dare, even to choose wrongly at times and
learn from our mistakes rather than being repeatedly pulled back from the
brink of using our own minds. For responsible religious adults, God is not
the authority telling them what to do. God is the divine power urging them
to grow, to reach, to dare. When God speaks to such people, He does not say,
as one might to a child, "I will be watching you to make sure you don't do
anything wrong." He says rather, "Go forth into an unchartered world where
you have never been before, struggle to find your path, but no matter what
happens, know that I will be with you."
   —*Harold Kushner*[6]

The opposite of faith is fear, not doubt. Doubt is an integral part of faith.
   —*Gene Owens*[7]

To think too long about doing a thing often becomes its undoing.
   —*Eva Young*[8]

Courage is resistance to fear, mastery of fear—not absence of fear. Except a
creature be part coward it is not a compliment to say it is brave.
   —*Mark Twain*[9]

Double-mindedness is wholly destructive of the Spiritual life. Totalitarian are
the claims of Christ.
   —*Thomas R. Kelly*[10]

Dear Lord,
   You call me forth again from the safety of my boat, and I seek to follow.
Stepping out into the unknown deep, I know that I will sink, that I will floun-
der and fail. I have done so many times. But you have always stood beside me,
picking me up, rescuing me from the folly of my own fears, and teaching me to
walk on the waters of faith.
   Help me to keep my eyes on you. May I not watch the towering waves and
the loving eyes of God at the same time. Give me singleness of vision and a love
of mystery. May I delight in knowing that when I follow you, the water will

always be over my head and the task will seem impossible. A great God would ask no less. Amen.

Questions among Friends

1. Do you sense that God is presently asking you to get out of your boat of familiarity and security and try something new? Is God asking you to plunge into waters over your head and trust him for success? Or is God simply asking you to do something that you've never done before—perhaps something that you have grave doubts about being able to accomplish? Share your thoughts with one another.

2. What are the towering waves that threaten you today? What are the worries and anxieties that you sometimes fear even God will not be able to help you overcome? What is it that takes your eyes off of faith and focuses them on fear?

3. Relate a time in your life when God was able to teach you some important lessons through a personal failure, a "sinking beneath the waves" experience. What were those lessons?

4. Share with the group a time when you responded in faith, threw caution to the wind, and decided to follow the lead of God. How did things turn out? What did you learn?

5. How do you think that God's Spirit is applying this particular story to your life today?

Chapter Five

THE MEANING OF WORDS

Jesus went out, along with His disciples, to the villages of Caesarea Philippi; and on the way He questioned His disciples, saying to them, "Who do people say that I am?" They told him, saying, "John the Baptist; and others say Elijah; but others, one of the prophets." He continued by questioning them, "But who do you say that I am?" Peter answered and said to Him, "You are the Christ." And He warned them to tell no one about Him." (Mark 8:27-30 [Matthew 16:13-16, Luke 9:18-21])

And Jesus said to him, "Blessed are you, Simon, Barjona, because flesh and blood did not reveal this to you, but My Father who is in heaven. (Matthew 16:17)

AFTER THE FEEDING OF THE FIVE THOUSAND AND THEIR ECSTATIC response, Jesus was no longer able to speak to large crowds. It was too dangerous. Now he turned primarily to teaching his own disciples, while avoiding volatile public situations.

After the stormy night at sea and Peter's attempt to walk on water, Jesus led the disciples away from the Sea of Galilee and slowly made his way twenty miles north to the region of Caesarea Philippi. Caesarea Philippi lies at the foot of Mount Hermon, the highest mountain in Israel and the source of the Jordan River. The city of Caesarea Philippi was pagan; devout Jews would not enter the city, only the region surrounding it. This is the farthest north Jesus is known to have traveled. For the moment he was safe from the political hotbed of Galilee.

The Meaning of Words

During this time of retreat, Jesus asked his disciples two direct and loaded questions. His first question was about public opinion. It went something like this: "You guys have spent a lot of time rubbing shoulders with the crowds. You hear a lot of things I never hear. So I'm curious. What are people saying about me? Who do they think that I am?"

The response from the disciples was straightforward: "Jesus, we are hearing three different opinions. Ever since John the Baptist was murdered by Herod, some are saying that you are his reincarnation, that his spirit has inhabited your body. Others are saying that you are the fulfillment of the ancient prophesy that Elijah will return before the coming of Messiah. The rest think you're another great prophet, a new one for our age. That's what we're hearing."

Then Jesus dropped the bomb: "Okay, that's what the crowds are saying. Now, what I really want to know is what the twelve of you are thinking? Who do *you* say that I am?"

Perhaps there was an awkward silence, and some of the disciples stared at their feet while others exchanged nervous glances. Then, the Gospel of Mark tells us, Peter spoke very simply: "You are the Christ," which, translated from Greek into Aramaic, means, "You are Messiah!"

Jesus then did a strange thing. He emphatically told his disciples that though Peter's words were true, they were to tell no one about him. They were not to announce to anybody that Jesus was Messiah. Why the insistence on secrecy?

The simple fact is that Peter had used the right word. Jesus was not a prophet. He was the promised Messiah. But Peter and his fellow disciples had no idea what the word *Messiah* truly meant. They were using a popular word loaded with all sorts of cultural imagery and popular mythology. But nobody—not Peter, not John, not even Caiaphas, the high priest—had a clue what the true meaning behind the word Messiah was all about.

In our lives today, we have learned to parrot religious words: God, Jesus, Holy Spirit, love, grace, sin, forgiveness, and the list goes on. But until we have had *personal experience* that makes these words come alive and take on deeper meaning, we do not know what we are talking about.

Sometimes it is a gut-wrenching and mind-numbing tragedy that knocks the hype off of words and makes us get down to the brass tacks of meaning. This is what the crucifixion and resurrection did for the disciples. It made them define the word *Messiah* in brand-new terms. But this was yet weeks away. It is earth-shaking events that shatter the walls of the overly familiar and make us search for meaning.

There is a small drinking fountain on the campus of the college that I attended, Furman University. I don't remember noticing the fountain as a student. It is a modest and unobtrusive font given by the classes of 1909, 1910, and 1911 in memory of Dr. John Todd Anderson. But while the fountain is simple, the story behind its dedication is powerful.

John Anderson was born in the small village of Woodruff, South Carolina in 1887. He was poor, but had a deep hunger for education. In 1905 he entered Furman University in Greenville, South Carolina, with a dream to become a doctor and a medical missionary. But his meager finances dwindled away, and he was forced to drop out of school. John found a job drilling water wells, determined to save enough money to go back to college.

A few years later John had drilled enough wells to return to school, this time at Wake Forest University in North Carolina. While at Wake Forest, he met Minnie Middleton, a student at neighboring Meredith College. Working diligently, John graduated from Wake Forest and then from the University of Louisville School of Medicine. John and Minnie married.

Wasting little time, John and Minnie were appointed as Baptist missionaries to China just as World War I erupted in Europe. They spent their first year in language school in Peking, and then moved to their permanent assignment at a hospital in Yangchow. At the age of thirty-one, all John's years of drilling wells, saving money, and going to school were finally coming together. John was at last fulfilling his dream.

Shortly after arriving in Yangchow, John had to attend a mission meeting in Shanghai. It was winter, and the weather was brutal. On the night of November 12, 1918, John clambered aboard a small sampan to cross the Yangtze River and catch a train on the other shore. In the middle of the river, a large steamer emerged out of a dense fog and sliced through the sampan. Dr. John Anderson, weighed down by winter clothes and an overcoat, was drowned.

Why? Why in God's name do such senseless tragedies happen? Why? Those were perhaps the precise words that Peter spoke when he saw thirty-three-year-old Jesus hideously tortured and crucified, writhing in pain, desperately hoping for the mercy of death to quickly come. "What does the word *Messiah* mean now?" Peter must have wondered. "Does it mean anything at all? A horrible mistake has been made somewhere! Messiahs don't die this way."

It was in this moment that the meaning of the word *Messiah* began to be transformed for Peter and all who followed Jesus. It was in these moments that the cryptic words of the ancient prophet, Isaiah, began to echo in their memories: "He [the Messiah] was despised and forsaken of men, a man of sorrows and acquainted with grief; . . . But He was pierced through for our transgressions, he was crushed for our iniquities; the chastening for our well-being fell upon Him; and by his scourging we are healed" (Isaiah 53:3-5).

Indeed, it was not until after the resurrection of Jesus that Isaiah's words had any meaning except to describe abject tragedy. But when the power of God raised Jesus from the dead, a new purpose was seen in suffering; a reason was revealed for the life, teachings, and example of Jesus. The word

Messiah now had fresh meaning for Peter, meaning that could never have been taught on a remote hillside in Galilee. The meaning had to be galvanized in Peter's soul through the hard knocks of personal experience.

Nearly a century ago, a small group of former students returned to Furman University to dedicate a water fountain to the memory of their friend Dr. John Todd Anderson. They did more than exhibit love for a departed friend; they were remembering the days when John Anderson drilled water wells to save money to go to school. Now, in the light of his sacrificial life and death, they were hearing again the words of Jesus as he sat by Jacob's well in Samaria and spoke to a troubled woman: "Everyone who drinks of this water will thirst again; but whoever drinks of the water that I will give him shall never thirst; but the water that I will give him will become in him a well of water springing up to eternal life" (John 4:13-14).

It takes years to understand simple words. It takes a lifetime of both experience and costly mistakes to dredge your soul deep enough to comprehend the depth of words like love and grace and forgiveness, and, yes, Messiah.

On the day that Peter blurted out, "You are the Christ," he had grasped the right word but the wrong meaning. And so Jesus said: "Keep it quiet. Let some time pass. Follow me a little longer. In time you will understand the words that you have spoken."

Truth above Reason

Approximately fifteen to twenty years after John Mark wrote the first account of Peter announcing that Jesus was the Messiah, the writer of the Gospel of Matthew was reading Mark's original version and added an additional footnote. Matthew alone tells us that after Peter's confession, Jesus said to Peter: "Blessed are you, Simon Barjona, because flesh and blood did not reveal this to you, but My Father who is in heaven."

The deeper meaning of spiritual words and concepts does not come to us only through years of living and the school of hard knocks. It also comes through those rare treasured moments when God's Spirit grants us insight far beyond our own intellect and wisdom. It is as if for a moment we intuit truth.

In a previous chapter, I mentioned the brilliant French mathematician Blaise Pascal, who was born in 1623 and soon recognized as a child prodigy. Indeed, his incredible ability to perceive mathematical truth and theory led many to believe that he was a savant. However, Pascal, a man of reason and intellect, was also a man who struggled with religious faith. Deep in his heart, Pascal sensed that there was a God; that spiritual truth exists. But unlike a mathematical formula, God cannot be placed on paper and proven. Agonizing over his own doubt and inability to firmly commit intellectually to belief in God, he wrote, "Seeing too much to deny and too little to be sure, I am in a state to be pitied."[1]

Yet Pascal also wrote of a moment later in his life when an unusual mystical experience brought him to firm belief in God. Late one night, when he was thirty-one years old—the age of Dr. John Anderson when he died in China—Pascal had a mystical experience in which he became emotionally convinced of the existence of God. Writing in his journal following his experience, Pascal penned one cogent sentence to describe the moment: "The God of Abraham, God of Isaac, God of Jacob, not the God of the philosophers and wise men." Pascal tore out the page, ripped open the lining of his coat, and sewed the page inside the lining. He did not want to ever be separated from this spiritual insight.

At its deepest level, faith in God is *suprarational* (not supernatural), meaning that faith is a multifaceted perception of truth that goes above and beyond reason. Faith is not irrational, for we must not put aside our intelligence and knowledge in order to believe. But the word *suprarational* does mean that truth is not limited to reason alone and that the total interplay of reason, emotion, intuition, and *spiritual insight* comes into the process of achieving religious faith. When Peter said, "You are the Christ," and Jesus answered, "Flesh and blood did not reveal this to you, but My Father who is in heaven," Jesus was saying that Peter spoke truth that cannot come by reason or formal education alone. Rather, such insight is a gift from God.

Yesterday, in a far less dramatic way, I had such an experience. I was walking down a deserted beach on Seabrook Island, South Carolina, totally alone with my thoughts. I was feeling a little dejected and lost. I began to pray out loud, as if God were walking beside me. I minced no words. I told God loudly and forcefully that sometimes I feel like I am talking to myself when I pray—that prayer often seems like my own mind game—and that I needed some reassurance that God was with me.

The sun was setting as I ranted and let God have both barrels of my frustration. Then I reached a sandy point where I ran out of island and ran out of beach. Breathless, I stopped and for the first time noticed the brilliant pastel colors of the incredible sunset. Just at that moment, a large, gray dolphin surfaced not ten feet off the shore in front of me. As his fin broke the water, I saw the notches on the crest and knew that this was an old fellow, a master of the years. Suddenly, in a mystical way, I knew—I simply knew—that God was with me. Tears sprang to my eyes, and the world danced in their prism. I realized that the epiphany of my smiling dolphin was like the burning bush for Moses, the wet and dry fleece for Gideon. From a source beyond reason, I was assured that the Spirit of God was with me. With Pascal, I knew that such knowledge was the knowledge of "the God of Abraham, God of Isaac, God of Jacob, not the God of the philosophers and wise men."

As quickly as the dolphin broke the surface, he disappeared. Like great ocean mammals, God does not appear on the surface of our awareness for long, but reenters the depths of the vast unknown. But it was enough. I sewed the memory in the lining of my thoughts and went on my way.

ALL CHRISTIANS SPEAK WORDS WITH MEANINGS THEY DO NOT KNOW. Our syllables sound like empty clichés or our own cultic language. But the language becomes real when we encounter the experiences that fill in the hollowness of the phonetic sound. When we have lived long enough to really sin, fail miserably, and be disappointed by ourselves and others, suddenly God's *grace* becomes more than a word. It is the best news we have ever heard! When we have been abused by life and hurt by friends, then we are confronted with what *forgiveness* really means. And when a good man like Dr. John Anderson dies, we are taught what the word *trust* really alludes to: to believe, in the midst of a world filled with tragedy, that our future is bathed in the light of purest goodness.

With Peter, we will spend our life learning the meaning of words. And it is often only when our bones have been broken and mended by time that words like *Messiah* and *Jesus* and *God* have much meaning.

Reflections
Proverbs 2:2-6, Proverbs 16:22, Jeremiah 29:12-13, 1 Corinthians 3:18-19, 13:9-12

Words realize nuthin'. They verify nuthin'. Unless you have suffered in your person the things the words describe.
　—*Mark Twain*[2]

There are sensitive periods or critical periods when a human being is especially able to learn quickly through certain types of experiences. Efforts at teaching, which would have been largely wasted if they had come earlier, give gratifying results when they come at the *teachable moment,* when the task should be learned.
　—*Robert J. Havighurst*[3]

It is easy to sit in discussion groups, to sit in a study and to read books, it is easy to discuss the intellectual truth of Christianity; but the essential thing is to experience the power of Christianity. And it is fatally easy to start at the

wrong end and to think of Christianity as something to be discussed, not as something to be experienced. It is certainly important to have an intellectual grasp of the orb of Christian truth; but it is still more important to have a vital experience of the power of Jesus Christ.
—*William Barclay*[4]

We must be like Jacob. We must wrestle with God. And Jacob wound up with a crippled hip. But he gained a blessing. And he would tell you it was worth the limp to know what he learned.
—*Grady Nutt*[5]

Only that which has happened to us can happen through us.
—*John Claypool*[6]

Dear Lord,

It is so easy for me to speak the language of Zion, to sprinkle my language with clichés that do not come from the heart. Teach me the true meaning of the great words of faith: mercy, justice, forgiveness, grace, and love. Reveal to me through my own experience a depth of knowledge that only comes from following Jesus. Amen.

Questions among Friends

1. Describe a moment in your life when one of the following words took on new meaning for you: grace, mercy, forgiveness, justice, faith, or trust. How did the words come to take on new meaning through your experience?

2. What does the ancient word *Messiah* mean to you? How would you explain this word to a person who had never heard it before?

Chapter Six

MARCHING ORDERS

And He began to teach them that the Son of Man must suffer many things and be rejected by the elders and the chief priests and the scribes, and be killed, and after three days rise again. And He was stating the matter plainly. And Peter took Him aside and began to rebuke Him. But turning around and seeing his disciples, he rebuked Peter and said, "Get behind Me, Satan; for you are not setting your mind on God's interests, but man's."

And He summoned the crowd with his disciples, and said to them, "If anyone wishes to come after Me, he must deny himself, and take up his cross and follow Me. For whoever wishes to save his life will lose it, but whoever loses his life for My sake and the gospel's will save it. For what does it profit a man to gain the whole world, and forfeit his soul? (Mark 8:31-37 [Matthew 16:21-26, Luke 9:2-27])

Only moments before, Peter had spoken the words, "You are the Messiah!" The echo of his excited voice still rang in Jesus' ears. Though Peter might not have comprehended what the word *Messiah* really meant, Jesus did.

Jesus was well aware that he had burned his bridges. There was no going back to a quiet carpenter's shop in Nazareth. He had already been violently thrown out of his hometown by an angry mob on charges of blasphemy. He was on Herod's wanted list for his close association with John the Baptist. And now the Jewish government, the Sanhedrin, was plotting against him. Arrest was inevitable. And once arrested, he knew he would meet the fate of his kinsman, John.

Such knowledge is an incredible weight for a man to bear alone. Turning to his disciples, Jesus let his guard down and allowed his thoughts to flow into words. And when he did—when he told them that he "must suffer many things and be rejected by the elders and the chief priests and the scribes, and be killed, and after three days rise again"—there was a stunned and unbelieving silence.

Finally, Peter, the same man who proclaimed him Messiah, took Jesus to the side and bluntly told him he was crazy. Peter rebuked Jesus, as Mark brusquely states. Peter told Jesus that he had no business becoming a martyr, and that his disciples wanted no part of it.

Jesus' jaw flinched. Peter's personal insensitivity hurt him, and his lack of insight angered him. Glaring hotly into that strong and impetuous fisherman's wide eyes, Jesus snapped, "Get behind Me, Satan, for you are not setting your mind on God's interests, but man's."

Those are strong words. And likely there was not a man alive except Jesus from whom Peter would have taken such words without a fight. Perhaps a strained silence followed—a time to cool off. And then Jesus turned and talked as directly as he had ever spoken to his disciples: "If anyone wishes to come after Me, he must deny himself, and take up his cross and follow Me. For whoever wishes to save his life will lose it, but whoever loses his life for My sake and the gospel's will save it. For what does it profit a man to gain the whole world, and forfeit his soul?"[1]

Jesus presented the marching orders for his followers in three short, staccato sentences. And anybody who contemplates being a disciple of Jesus' had better listen. Nowhere does Jesus speak clearer than he does here.

"He Must Deny Himself, and Take Up His Cross . . ."

Jesus did not use the word *cross* lightly. Two thousand years later, Christians are so blithely familiar with this word that it bears little impact. But to Jesus and his disciples, the specter of a cross struck terror in their souls. Crucifixion was the most dreaded of fates. And Jesus was saying to his followers, "If you follow me, you had better be ready to be crucified."

The fact is that to be a Christian is often a dangerous risk. Most American Christians are shamefully unaware of the fact that more Christians were martyred for their faith in the twentieth century than in any century since the life of Jesus. Though Americans are protected from religious tyranny and persecution by our Constitution, most of the world does not have such privilege.

A man whose memory often goads my thoughts is a young German minister and theologian named Dietrich Bonhoeffer. Sadly his heroic story is quickly fading into the shadows in the minds of present-day Christians. But his life must not be forgotten.

Dietrich Bonhoeffer was born in Breslau, Germany, in 1906. His father was a physician, and later, a professor of psychiatry at the University of Berlin. His mother descended from a long line of well-known scholars. Young Dietrich was raised in a family of privilege, influence, and distinction.

By age sixteen Dietrich had decided to become a minister within the Protestant church in Germany. At age seventeen he began his university studies to prepare for ministry. He was a brilliant student and quickly distinguished himself for independent thought and cogent insights. He completed his doctoral studies by age twenty-four, and was offered a faculty position teaching theology at the University of Berlin.

Prior to beginning his teaching career, however, Bonhoeffer pursued postdoctoral studies at Union Theological Seminary in New York. He made many friends among the American faculty before his return to Germany. In 1931 he began teaching at the University of Berlin, and in 1932 national elections ushered Adolf Hitler and his Nazi party into power.

Bonhoeffer quickly saw the danger imposed on the Christian Church by Nazi ideology. He denounced both the spirit and the teachings of the Nazi party. On August 5, 1936, he was informed that he could no longer teach at the University of Berlin due to his political views. By the age of thirty, he was a marked man.

Bonhoeffer was soon asked by the leadership of the Confessing Church in Germany—a remnant of the German Protestant Church that opposed Hitler—to assume the leadership of a small, illegal seminary that would train ministers to lead underground churches. He did so for three years, until 1939, when he encountered a crisis. As Germany crushed Poland and then declared war on France and England, Bonhoeffer was faced with mandatory military service. His friends at Union Seminary in New York knew of his dilemma and offered him a faculty position. Bonhoeffer seized this lifeline and sailed to New York.

Soon after his arrival, however, Bonhoeffer was besieged with doubt and guilt concerning his decision. He wrote to his good friend and fellow professor at Union Seminary, Reinhold Niebuhr, and shared his perplexity:

> I shall have no right to participate in the reconstruction of Christian life in Germany after the war if I do not share the trials of this time with my people. . . . Christians in Germany will face the terrible alternative of either willing the defeat of their nation in order that Christian civilization may survive, or willing the victory of their nation and thereby destroying our civilization. I know which of these alternatives I must choose; but I cannot make this choice in security.[2]

Within six weeks Bonhoeffer made his decision to return to Germany. He could not leave German Christians to face Nazi persecution and not be with them. At age thirty-three—the same age at which Jesus was crucified—Bonhoeffer picked up his own cross and faced Golgotha.

Arriving in Germany, Bonhoeffer was immediately informed that he could no longer speak publicly anywhere within the German Reich. At the same time, Bonhoeffer became increasingly aware of the lunacy of Hitler and the atrocities being committed against millions of Jews, Gypsies, and other innocent people. It became clear to Bonhoeffer that Adolf Hitler must be removed from power for the sake of Germany and the future of the world.

Bonhoeffer was approached by some prominent German citizens and military leaders to join a resistance movement. The movement's purpose was to remove Hitler from power, possibly by assassination. With deep regret and mixed emotions, Bonhoeffer offered his cooperation. Months later, when an assassination attempt was carried out and an injured Hitler narrowly escaped with his life, Bonhoeffer and other resistance leaders were implicated. Arrested on the same week that he was publicly engaged to be married to Maria von Wedemeyer, he was imprisoned for eighteen long months.

As Allied armies surged across the borders of Germany, and Russian troops converged on Berlin, Bonhoeffer's hopes soared. However, on the dawn of a gray morning, when Allied artillery could be heard booming in the distance, a soldier appeared at Bonhoeffer's cell door and called out his name. Bonhoeffer was taken to the gallows and hanged for treason, only days before the war ended. His final recorded words, spoken minutes before his death, were, "This is the end—for me the beginning of life."[3]

To be a Christian is to understand that our faith often demands a high cost from us. And this cost should be paid not just by a few Christians faced with tragic circumstances, but by all Christians. Now, does this mean that every Christian should seek martyrdom? Not at all. What it does mean is that being a Christian should cost us in terms of our time, our priorities, our care for others, our money, and in some circumstances, our life.

I find it interesting that most Christians in America do not take seriously the Old Testament teaching that we should give a minimum of 10 percent of our income to God, to share our money to help others in the name and spirit of Jesus Christ. It is a simple fact that if all Christians gave a tenth of their income every year to help others, much of the world's hunger, disease, poverty, and human suffering could be wiped out in less than a century. But few are willing to literally pay this cost.

What if every Christian took seriously the idea that his or her vocation, whatever it may be, is a means to do ministry, to be the presence of Christ in the life of everyone with whom we professionally interact? Yes, it would cost us something. It would cost us time and involvement. It would thrust us into situations that we would just as soon avoid. It would cause us to be far more sensitive to the needs of others and to discover ways that we could help them. It would be costly.

It may come as a surprise to many to realize that Christianity is not just a doctrine or an ethical code to live by. Christianity is not primarily focused on going to church to worship God. Christianity is not an egocentric way to enrich and empower our own spiritual lives. Rather, Jesus emphatically tells us that to follow him is above all a costly personal journey of self-sacrifice and that we will shed blood, sweat, and tears.

Dietrich Bonhoeffer looked out of a prison window at a world crazed by war and realized that most Christians had accepted "cheap grace." Their faith had cost them little. And as a result, the devil's own holocaust was enveloping the world.

Losing Your Life to Save Your Life

There is strong paradox in Jesus' words. After he informs his disciples that following his example will be costly, he suddenly turns on his ironic heel and declares: "For whoever wishes to save his life will lose it, but whoever loses his life for My sake and the gospel's, will save it. For what does it profit a man to gain the whole world, and forfeit his soul?"

At first blush it would seem that Jesus is simply saying: "Don't worry if you die. You've got eternal life insurance. Die for my sake, and you'll get your reward in heaven." But this is not what Jesus is saying. While not denying the joy and happiness of eternal life that comes through salvation, Jesus is primarily saying: "If you are ever going to find happiness—real happiness—on this earth, it is only going to come when you quit trying to save your life, control your life, rule your life, and instead you give your life away. When you lose your life, then you find your life. When you give your life away, then you receive it back sevenfold."

A few weeks after this, Jesus explained further. A young man who was independently wealthy and in firm control of his life and dreams came to see Jesus. He knelt before Jesus and sincerely asked, "Good Teacher, what shall I do to inherit eternal life?" Jesus knew that the man was a devout and orthodox Jew. And so he replied, "One thing you lack: go, sell all you possess and give to the poor, and you will have treasure in heaven; and come, follow Me." The story concludes that the young man departed very upset, because he could not bear to give up his possessions (Mark 10:17-22).

It is important to note that nowhere else in the New Testament does Jesus ask a person to go and sell all that he has in order to follow him. He did not ask Peter to do this. Peter still owned his boats and fishing business. Jesus himself did not do this. But Jesus knew this young man's weakness—that he was not willing to pay the cost of discipleship—and revealed his spiritual Achilles' heel.

Later, Peter evaluated his own situation in light of this rich young man who could not abandon his possessions. Peter, in contrast, had left his wife, his house, his profession, and his comfortable lifestyle to follow Jesus. Perhaps in a spirit of self-pity, or in hope of reward, Peter blurted out to Jesus, "Behold, we have left everything, and followed You." Jesus' response was not what Peter expected: "Truly I say to you, there is no one who has left house or brothers or sisters or mother or father or children or farms, for My sake and for the gospel's sake, but that he will receive a hundred times as much *now in the present age,* houses and brothers and sisters and mothers and children and farms, along with persecutions; and in the world to come, eternal life (Mark 10:28-30, emphasis added).

Jesus' point is clear. The only way to close out our years with a full heart and rich memories is to have lived a life of sacrificial love for others. When we do this, every man we love becomes our brother; everyone woman we assist becomes our sister. When we enter into Christian fellowship, our family increases exponentially. And in the strangest of ways, when we give our possessions away to others, our world increases in richness.

This is one of the greatest paradoxes of Christianity: when you lose it, you gain it; when you surrender control, you gain control; when you finally die to self, then you truly find freedom. These are not the ways of our world. But they are the ways of what Jesus called "the kingdom of God." Embracing this paradox is the only way to find happiness this side of heaven.

NOW, BACK TO THE ORIGINAL SCENE. WHEN JESUS TOLD HIS DISCIPLES, "I am going to have to die to stay true to My calling from God," Peter lost it, exploded, and rebuked Jesus. This courageous fisherman could give up everything to follow Jesus, but he was not willing to watch Jesus die or to relinquish his own life. Jesus responded simply: "If anyone wishes to come after Me, he must deny himself, and take up his cross and follow Me. For whoever wishes to save his life will lose it, but whoever loses his life for My sake and the gospel's will save it."

It would take Peter longer than a lifetime to understand these words. It will take us a long time too. These are our marching orders. As Christians we must follow and bear our cross with Jesus.

Reflections
Micah 6:6-8, Matthew 10:34-39, John 12:23-27

The cross is laid on every Christian. The first Christ-suffering which every man must experience is the call to abandon the attachments of this world. . . . As we embark upon discipleship we surrender ourselves to Christ in union with his death—we give over our lives to death. Thus it begins; the cross is not the terrible end to an otherwise God-fearing life, but it meets us at the beginning of our communion with Christ. When Christ calls a man, he bids him come and die.
    —*Dietrich Bonhoeffer*[4]

When a man really gives up trying to make something out of himself—a saint, or a converted sinner, or a churchman (a so-called clerical somebody), a righteous or unrighteous man. . . .When in the fullness of tasks, questions, success or ill-hap, experiences and perplexities, a man throws himself into the arms of God . . . then he wakes with Christ in Gethsemane. That is faith.
    ——*Dietrich Bonhoeffer*[5]

The command of Jesus is hard, unutterably hard, for those who try to resist it. But for those who willingly submit, the yoke is easy, and the burden is light. "His commandments are not grievous" (1 John 5:3). The commandment of Jesus is not a sort of spiritual shock treatment. Jesus asks nothing of us without giving us the strength to perform it. His commandment never seeks to destroy life, but to foster, strengthen and heal it.
    —*Dietrich Bonhoeffer*[6]

The only man who has the right to say that he is justified by grace alone is the man who has left all to follow Christ. Such a man knows that the call to discipleship is a gift of grace, and that the call is inseparable from the grace. But those who try to use this grace as a dispensation from following Christ are simply deceiving themselves.
    —*Dietrich Bonhoeffer*[7]

Most people are bothered by those passages in Scripture which they cannot understand; but as for me, I always noticed that the passages in Scripture which troubled me most are those that I do understand.
    —*Mark Twain*[8]

If a man has not found something worth giving his life for, he is not fit to live.
    —*Martin Luther King Jr.*[9]

Dear Father,

Enable me to see the cross of service that is mine this day. Help me to not shrink from sacrifice. May I discover the purpose for which I have come to this hour. Amen.

Questions among Friends

1. Describe a time when making a personal sacrifice for someone else brought you great joy or satisfaction.

2. Can you remember a moment when you hesitated or refused to "pay the cost of discipleship"?

3. How can you best describe your "marching orders" at this time in your life? How do you think God is asking you to serve him? Will your service require a cost or a sacrifice?

4. How can your friends best pray for you in this moment of your life? Where do you need strength, courage, and wisdom to bear your cross?

Chapter Seven

A VISION IN THE NIGHT

Six days later, Jesus took with Him Peter and James and John, and brought them up on a high mountain by themselves. And He was transfigured before them; and His garments became radiant and exceedingly white, as no launderer on earth can whiten them. Elijah appeared to them along with Moses; and they were talking with Jesus. Peter said to Jesus, "Rabbi, it is good for us to be here; let us make three tabernacles, one for You, and one for Moses, and one for Elijah." For he did not know what to answer; for they became terrified. Then a cloud formed overshadowing them, and a voice came out of the cloud, "This is My beloved Son, listen to Him!" All at once they looked around and saw no one with them anymore, except Jesus alone. (Mark 9:2-8 [Matthew 17:1-8, Luke 9:28-36])

SIX DAYS AFTER PETER DECLARED THAT JESUS WAS THE MESSIAH, Jesus took Peter, James, and John and climbed to the top of a high mountain in the region of Caesarea Philippi. The mountain was likely Mount Hermon, which is 9,200 feet high, the tallest mountain in Israel. While in this transcendent setting, an unusual and significant event transpired in the life of Jesus.

Luke alone intimates that the scene took place at night when he states that the three disciples "had been overcome with sleep" (Mark 9:32). In darkness they were awakened to stare unbelieving at a scene they could not comprehend. Perhaps huddled in blankets around a dimming fire, they gazed at Jesus, and realized that he looked different. His skin seemed to glow, and Mark relates that "His garments became radiant and exceedingly white, as no launderer on earth can whiten them." Most mysteriously, Jesus was talking to two men they had never seen before. Though they were not introduced, Peter, James, and John instantly knew that they were the ancient figures of Moses and Elijah. As if in a dream state, they instinctively recognized these historical giants who were now gathered before them.

What was happening? How do we explain this mystical occurrence? Only the writer of the Gospel of Matthew gives us insight into the nature of this scene. Some fifteen to twenty years after the writing of Mark's Gospel, the author of the Gospel of Matthew used Mark's Gospel as a primary source for writing his own Gospel. As he described this mountaintop story, he followed closely the wording of Mark's earlier account, making his own editorial changes and emphasis from time to time. In Matthew 17:9, the author deliberately expands Mark's succinct version, and writes, "As they were coming down from the mountain, Jesus commanded them, saying, 'Tell the vision to no one.'" Matthew intentionally selected a technical Greek word, *orama,* to express the word *vision.* Orama usually means "a supernatural vision," regardless of whether the person who has the vision is asleep or awake.[1] Thus the writer of Matthew perceived—and emphasized—that what took place on the mountain was not that Moses and Elijah physically descended from heaven, but rather that Jesus and his three disciples shared in a God-inspired *vision* in which Moses and Elijah appeared. Such an understanding of this event does not discount the miraculous, for the shared perception of a vision is as miraculous as if Moses and Elijah had appeared in the flesh. However, the word chosen by the writer of Matthew does help us to understand the nature of what probably transpired on the mountaintop.

Insight into the Future

What was the importance of this vision to Jesus and his three disciples? What did the vision mean? Only the Gospel of Luke tells us what Jesus, Moses, and Elijah were discussing. Luke writes, "And behold, two men were talking with Him; and they were Moses and Elijah, who, appearing in glory, were speaking of His departure which He was about to accomplish at Jerusalem" (9:30-31). Thus, in this dark moment of the night, the vision was casting light on the immediate future that was confronting Jesus and his disciples. Moses and Elijah—representing the authority of the "Law and the Prophets"—were confirming that the end of Jesus' life was drawing near and that his visit to Jerusalem at Passover would result in his "departure."

Like the disciples of old, we walk in darkness most of our lives, unsure of what the future holds. We may have hopes, dreams, and intimations of what tomorrow will bring, but we seldom have a clear picture. Yet, we do have mountaintop experiences when, for a brief moment, light flashes across our midnight path, and we see with clarity the next step along our way. As disciples of Jesus, we learn that God—at the proper time—is always faithful to show us the way.

I remember the day that I was married. I was exuberant. I was also scared. Beth and I had pooled our savings and had the grand sum of one hundred and ten dollars between us. We were moving from Georgia to Kentucky to attend seminary. And to be honest, I was not sure at that time whether seminary was right for me. But as I stood arm in arm with Beth before God's altar, I heard the minister say: "You cannot know now what the future holds. Yet, you can know now that you face the future together, secure in each other's love and surrounded by the care of your Good Shepherd." Suddenly the darkness lifted. I could see the next few steps along our path. I knew that God walked with us. On many future days, I would look back to this holy moment and repeat those words for reassurance as I walked again down a darkened path.

I also remember a moment several years ago when I went to the hospital to visit Dr. Abner McCall, a former president of Baylor University. Dr. McCall grew up in an orphanage. There were many days in his youth when he did not know where life was leading or how he could possibly become successful. But his brilliant mind, caring personality, and Christian faith led him toward academic success, a brilliant career in law, and leadership of his alma mater, Baylor University.

As Dr. McCall and I talked, I could tell that this elderly man knew that the end of his life was near. Despite his sickness and the gravity of the moment, our conversation soon turned to a familiar topic: favorite books and poetry. Dr. McCall had an unusual ability to memorize long passages of poetry, and age had not robbed him of this gift. With a gleam in his quiet eyes, Dr. McCall looked at me and said, "Scott, let me share with you perhaps my favorite poem, by Alfred Noyes." It was called "Journey by Night." Growing quiet, it seemed he reached far back into his childhood, collecting his words, reading again the lines from a teenage journal, savoring words that had directed his life. Softly he intoned:

Thou who never canst err, for Thyself are the Way;
Thou whose infinite kingdom is flooded with day;
Thou whose eyes behold all, for Thyself art the light,
Look down on us gently who journey by night.

By the pity, revealed in Thy loneliest hour,
Forsaken, self-bound and self-emptied of power;
Thou who, even in death, hadst all heaven in sight,
Look down on us gently who journey by night.

On the road to Emmaus, they thought Thou wast dead;
Yet they saw Thee and knew Thee in the breaking of bread.

Though the day was spent, in Thy face there was light.
Look down on us gently who journey by night.[2]

Today I can still hear the cadence of Dr. McCall's words, an orphan's voice in the night. This poem was obviously his credo. Throughout his long journey, he had learned that God does look down on us gently through our darkness, and lends us his light. A few days later, Dr. McCall died. He had faithfully accomplished his departure in Jerusalem.

Peter would learn during the course of his years that he frequently walked in darkness, unsure of what the future would hold. But he never forgot the vision in the night, the light on Jesus' face, the confirmation through Moses and Elijah that God was leading Jesus to Jerusalem and would provide for his needs. The ability to trust God for our future is a crucial lesson for Christian disciples.

The Desire to Capture the Moment

When Peter awoke to confront the mystic vision, his bleary mind was drugged by sleep. It was near the time of the Feast of Tabernacles, and perhaps Peter had been thinking of a popular Jewish custom, established in Leviticus 23:39-44, in which a Jewish family would make a small tabernacle (or tent) of interlacing tree branches and live in it during the seven-day period of the Feast of Tabernacles. The festive tabernacles symbolized the Jewish hope that one day God would literally return and "pitch his tent" with his chosen people, just as he had when the original tabernacle was first erected and transported during the forty years of wandering in the wilderness. It is possible that as Peter drifted off to sleep that night, he was thinking of his own family and the fact that they had not yet built their tabernacle.[3]

Now, when Peter awoke to suddenly encounter the vision, his mind was still dreaming of building a tabernacle. The Gospel of Mark tells us that as the vision began to fade and Elijah and Moses disappeared, Peter sleepily blurted out, "Rabbi, it is good for us to be here; let us make three tabernacles, one for You, and one for Moses, and one for Elijah." Then Mark adds, "For [Peter] did not know what to answer." Though his mind was muddled, Peter intended to keep the vision from ending, to prolong a glorious spiritual moment, to keep Moses and Elijah with them a little longer.

Many of us can relate to Peter's feelings. From time to time, as Christians we experience a moment when God seems to be particularly close. It's as if for a few fleeting moments, a veil is lifted and we see God's purposes more clearly. We literally feel the presence of God embrace us, and we do not want the experience to fade away.

Several years ago my family and I were on vacation in Estes Park, Colorado, nestled high in the Rocky Mountains. Our family had spent the afternoon hiking on some of the most beautiful trails I have ever seen. Yet my mind was distracted from the scenery by a momentous decision with which I was struggling. I knew that soon I might be offered a job that would be challenging and compelling. I did not know how to respond. And the more I analyzed the pros and the cons of the decision, the more confused and anxious I felt.

Late that night after our three children had gone to bed, I left our cabin to take a walk. Even in August the air was cool and bracing. Gazing up through a canopy of evergreen branches, I could see that there was not a cloud in the sky. The darkness was so dense that the sky looked three-dimensional, and the stars shone with staccato brilliance. The high altitude made the heavens effervescent.

Standing still, I searched for the constellations that I could recognize. The Big Dipper tilted nearly upside down in its arc across the heavens. For a moment I was transfixed. Without conscious thought I was suddenly infused with the glory and majesty of God. A peace came over me that made my vocational decision look small. I knew that God was in control of my life. I knew that the Lord was my Shepherd, and that "surely goodness and lovingkindness will follow me all the days of my life, and I will dwell in the house of the LORD forever" (Psalm 23:6).

Standing in the silence I wanted the moment never to end. I dreaded moving a muscle, thinking a thought, taking a step toward home. I did not want the moment to go away, the vision to fade.

The reality, however, is that such moments are treasures to behold for a brief time, and then they must be returned to the vault of our memory. The night ends. The stars dim. A child cries. And we must return to the world. We must descend the mountain. We must continue toward our own Jerusalem, whose walls encompass turmoil, anxiety, grief, pain, and the gnawing fear of the unknown. We cannot capture the fleeting vision of goodness with our eyes, our hands, our hearts, or even the shelter of a tabernacle.

With Peter, each Christian disciple learns to discern a correct sextant reading from the height of the mountain and the nearness of the stars, and then we must proceed boldly down the hillside into the unknown. The clarity of the mountaintop vision must sometimes last us a long time. We must hold on to its course—be true to the direction of the vision—when later we fear that we are lost, that God has forsaken us, that on the mountaintop of yesterday we were only misguided, quixotic fools. We cannot prolong the moment of divine inspiration. We can only keep the vision in our mind and be guided by its light.

Words of Confirmation

As the vision faded, the disciples and Jesus were enveloped in a dense, cold cloud that often enshrouds the slopes of Mount Hermon, even today. In this cool, swirling fog, they heard a voice that said, "This is My beloved Son, listen to Him!" It was the same voice that Jesus heard declare at his baptism, "You are My beloved Son, in You I am well-pleased" (Mark 1:11). In both instances God was affirming his unique relationship with Jesus of Nazareth. This was a confirmation (or reaffirmation), in the middle of Jesus' ministry, that his Father was still with him—continuing to love him, inspire him, and direct his way.

All of us need to hear such words of confirmation from time to time. When we grow weary and the world seems to be more than we can handle, we long to be reassured that God is with us. It is in those moments that we want to be surrounded by "the cloud of God" and hear our Father's words: "Listen to Jesus! When you've lost your way, listen to Jesus!"

I have been a pastor for twenty-eight years. I have many more years of ministry ahead of me. Yet at midlife I sometimes grow discouraged. I become disillusioned with the Church, with the flock that I lead, with myself. It's easy at the midpoint of life to want to throw in the towel.

Perhaps it was at the midpoint of ministry that Peter also wanted to climb down from the mountain and go back to Galilee and his fishing boat. In the lonely darkness of the night, he longed to retreat home and build that special tent for his family to live in and celebrate the joy of the holy season together. But the voice of God comes again and again to Christian disciples, and commands, "This is My beloved Son, listen to Him!"

And what does Jesus tell us? "Come, follow me! Follow me to the mountaintops and through the valleys. Follow me in the good times and the bad times. But most of all, follow me to Jerusalem. For it is in Jerusalem that you must be crucified with me and raised with me to new life. You cannot know me if you do not follow me. Trust that I am the way, and the truth, and the life!"

And so, with the voice from the cloud ringing in their terrified minds, Peter, James, and John descended Mount Hermon with Jesus to rejoin the other nine disciples and begin again their march toward Jerusalem. Though the vibrant vision had revived their flagging souls, they comprehended little and had much more to learn. And so Mark concludes this story: "[Jesus] gave them orders not to relate to anyone what they had seen, until the Son of Man rose from the dead. They seized upon that statement, discussing with one another what rising from the dead meant" (9:9-10). For not even a vision in the night nor the witness of Moses and Elijah could possibly foretell the power and the meaning of the death and resurrection of Jesus.

Reflections
Exodus 19:16-20, Exodus 34:27-30, Psalm 77:18-20, Psalm 139:7-12

A glimpse is not a vision. But to a man on a mountain road by night, a glimpse of the next three feet of road may matter more than a vision of the horizon.
—*C. S. Lewis*[4]

God often gives in one brief moment that which he has for a long time denied.
—*Thomas à Kempis*[5]

He leadeth me! O blessed tho't! O words with heav'nly comfort fraught!
Whate'er I do, where'er I be, still tis God's hand that leadeth me!

Lord, I would clasp Thy hand in mine, Nor ever murmur nor repine,
Content, whatever lot I see, since tis Thy hand that leadeth me!

And when my task on earth is done, when, by Thy grace, the vict'ry's won,
E'en death's cold wave I will not flee, since God thro' Jordan leadeth me!

He leadeth me, He leadeth me, by His own hand He leadeth me:
His faithful foll'wer I would be, for by His hand He leadeth me.
—*Joseph H. Gilmore*[6]

Dear Father,

There are nights when I jolt awake, startled. The world is dark and my mind is foggy. I see no light, and I cannot find my way. I am frightened by what I cannot see.

I need a vision, Lord, a guiding light by which to see the path before me. I need a clarity of purpose, a mission to live for, a cause worthy of my life. But most of all, I need to be reassured that amidst the dimness of my world, you walk with me.

Lord, for a moment take me to a mountaintop and help me glimpse a promised land. Let me hear your voice stir me to obedience. Give me the courage to venture toward my own Jerusalem and bear my cross. And may I believe that behind all pain and loss is resurrection and new life. Amen.

Questions among Friends

1. Describe a "mountaintop experience" in your life, when light was cast on your darkened path and you glimpsed a sure direction or vision for your future.

2. Share with your friends a time when you felt especially close to God, and you did not want the spiritual moment to fade away.

3. What hopes and dreams do you have for your future? How do you feel that God is leading you in this chapter of your life? Is there a "Jerusalem" ahead of you that you are trying to find the courage to face?

4. In recent days, has your life been characterized more as being high on a mountain, stuck on a flat plateau, or slogging through a deep, dark valley?

5. Choose a person in your group, and share what your prayer is for them and for their future.

Chapter Eight

"WHAT'S IN IT FOR ME?"

As He was setting out on a journey, a man ran up to Him and knelt before Him, and asked Him, "Good Teacher, what shall I do to inherit eternal life?" . . . Looking at him, Jesus felt a love for him, and said to him, "One thing you lack: go and sell all you possess and give it to the poor, and you will have treasure in heaven; and come, follow Me." But at these words he was saddened, and he went away grieving, for he was one who owned much property.

Peter began to say to Him, "Behold, we have left everything and followed You." Jesus said, "Truly I say to you, there is no one who has left house or brothers or sisters or mother or father or children or farms, for My sake and for the gospel's sake, but that he will receive a hundred times as much now in the present age, houses and brothers and sisters and mothers and children and farms, along with persecutions; and in the age to come, eternal life. But many who are first will be last, and the last, first." (Mark 10:17, 21-22, 28-31 [Matthew 19:27-30, Luke 18:27-30])

AS THIS SCENE OPENS, PETER HAS HEARD AN INTERESTING CONVERSATION between Jesus and a wealthy young man. The man was winsome and devout, and had come to Jesus to ask an earnest question: "What shall I do to inherit eternal life?" Jesus answered him with a requirement that he had not demanded of Peter or any other disciple. Recognizing a deep-seated weakness in this young man, Jesus said, "Go and sell all you possess and give it to the poor." The man was shattered because he could not bring himself to obey Jesus. He walked away dejected and grieved.

Why was this man unable to obey Jesus? The most obvious answer is that he loved his possessions more than he loved Jesus. As a result, he could not allow following Jesus to be the highest priority in his life. This answer is no doubt correct. But a second and more spiritually crippling problem lurks behind the young man's dilemma.

What does the young man ask for? He wants to receive "eternal life." On the surface nothing is wrong with this quest. The desire to experience eternal life is a deep and primal hunger for each of us. Note, however, that the young man does not ask: "Jesus, how can I follow you? How can I be your disciple? How can I serve you and my neighbor?" Rather, the emphasis of his question is centered around *his own reward*—"How can *I* obtain eternal life?" In this gripping scene, we see that the quest for personal reward is a spiritual pitfall for most Christian disciples.

Our Desire for Reward

As the story continues, Mark soon shows us that Peter does not escape the same temptation to seek personal reward. After watching the wealthy fellow turn and walk away, Peter reflected on his own situation. He had left much behind to follow Jesus. He had left his wife in Capernaum, his fishing boat beached by the Sea of Galilee, and now he was risking his reputation—if not his life—to be a disciple of Jesus. Looking at the other disciples who had also abandoned much, Peter suddenly turned and said to Jesus, "Behold, we have left everything and followed You." The implication is clear: "Now, Jesus, for those of us who have been faithful to follow you, what is our reward? What's in it for me?"[1]

I remember when this crisis point in Christian discipleship first jumped up and bit me. I was a freshman in college, and had just met Hans Zimmer, a new foreign exchange student from Germany. The son of a university philosophy professor, Hans had inherited his father's brilliance and curiosity. Reared in the midst of stimulating intellectual conversations, my German friend loved nothing more than to plunge into the spirited bull sessions that often took place in our dorm rooms late at night.

One evening several of my friends and I were studying in my room for a religion exam. Bleary-eyed, we looked up at midnight as Hans sauntered in and flopped down on the bed, blue eyes sparkling and wide grin glowing. Hans was ready to launch into a heavy debate, and religion was fair game.

I already knew that Hans was not a Christian. He had told me that though he respected my faith, he just could not believe in a God "who could allow the suffering that I have seen in this world." Many times we had talked about this thorny ethical problem—why bad things happen to innocent people—and Hans's critical mind had caused me to dig deeper and wrestle with this legitimate theological question.

Now, sipping a cola, Hans took another tact. "Hey, you guys, tell me something. If there was no promise of heaven, do you think many Christians would be hanging around? I mean, if the Bible simply taught that you're supposed to lead a good life like Jesus did, and then when you

die, well, you just die and it's all over, . . . do you think you would still want
to be good Christian boys and girls?" *Would we do it if there is no reward*

Hans hit a home run that night, and his question nailed me. Long past
that evening, Hans's proposition haunted me: "Why am I a Christian? Is it
for personal reward? Why should I seek to love my neighbor and live by
Jesus' teachings? Am I doing this just to pass muster and punch my ticket
into heaven? Do I, like the rich young man, want only to know what I must
do to inherit eternal life?"

Perhaps insight into resolving this question can be seen in the life of
another rich young man named Francis Xavier. Francis was born in 1506 to
Dr. Joao de Jasso and Maria d' Aspilcueta, at Xavier castle in Navarra, Spain.
The youngest of six children, Francis was surrounded from birth with wealth
and luxury.

When he was eighteen, Francis left home to study at the University of
Paris. His two roommates were Christians, and Francis began to observe how
they lived out their faith. One of his friends, Ignatius Loyola, often quoted
passages of scripture to Francis. Jesus' words, "What does it profit a man to
gain the whole world if he loses his own soul?" lodged in Francis's mind.
Pressed by this concern for his own salvation, Francis became a Christian and
began to mature in his commitment to Christ. Before graduation Francis
and his friends formed a religious society—the Society of Jesus—that later
became known as the Jesuits.

Francis was ordained a priest at age thirty-one. Four years later he was
sent to the East Indies as a missionary, by the invitation of the king of
Portugal. During the next eleven years, his ministries took him to India, Sri
Lanka, Malaysia, Indonesia, China, and Japan. Despite chronic seasickness
and declining health, Francis felt a desperate drive to bring the Gospel to as
many places as possible.

One day in the midst of a voyage, a matured Francis Xavier reflected on
his life—what he had left behind to follow Jesus—and wrote a sonnet that
addressed the questions: "Why am I a Christian? Why do I obey and serve
Jesus Christ? Why do I love God?" These are his words:

> My God, I love Thee;
> Not because I hope for heaven thereby,
> Nor yet because who love Thee not
> Must die eternally.

> Thou, O my Jesus,
> Thou didst me upon the cross embrace;
> For me didst bear the nails and spear
> And manifold disgrace.

Why, then why, O blessed Jesus Christ,
Should I not love Thee well?
Not for the hope of winning heaven,
Or of escaping hell;
Not with the hope of gaining aught,
Not seeking a reward.

But as Thyself hast loved me,
O Everlasting Lord,
E'en so I love Thee, and will love,
And in Thy praise will sing;
Solely because Thou art my God,
And my Eternal King.[2]

Shortly after writing these words, Francis Xavier died of a fever on St. John's Island while traveling to China. During his forty-six years, Francis had slowly matured to understand that Christian discipleship and obedience to God is based not on the promise of personal reward, but rather is spawned from sheer gratitude and love for what God has done for us.

Peter also would learn this lesson. Though he begins in this scene by asking Jesus, "What's in it for me?" and boldly seeks reward, Peter's reason for following Jesus would change before he died as a martyr approximately thirty-five years later in Rome. By the end of his life, Peter's desire to obey and follow Jesus would be motivated by a deep love for his Master, who lived and died for Peter's sake.

And so it must be for each of us. We may begin our Christian journey out of a singular desire to secure our own salvation. We may serve God and love our neighbor primarily out of parental obedience, social obligation, or the teachings of the Church. But sooner or later, we will realize that only one thing will enable us to be faithful Christians over the long course of our life. That one thing is the slow development of our own love for God, which is nurtured through years of living. If we live long enough and deep enough, we will know what the aging Apostle John meant when he wrote, "We love, because He first loved us" (1 John 4:19).

The Promise of Reward

Now we must look at the other side of the paradox. Though we cannot seek to be disciples of Jesus out of the motive of personal reward, nevertheless, if we do follow Jesus, we will receive great and wonderful gratification. Listen to Jesus' promise: "Truly I say to you, there is no one who has left house or brothers or sisters or mother or father or children or farms, for My sake and for the gospel's sake, but that he will receive a hundred times as much now in the present age, houses and brothers and sisters and mothers and children and farms, along with persecutions; and in the age to come, eternal life" (Mark 10:29-30).

This promise of Jesus' can be seen in the history of my own family. Nearly fifty years ago, my parents felt that God's Spirit was leading them to become missionaries and teachers in the Philippine Islands. My mother was thirty-five years old and excited about this prospect. However, her mother— my grandmother—soon poured cold water on my mother's aspirations.

My grandmother had slowly become a bitter woman as she advanced in age. During the years she had lost many things: a husband to divorce, financial security to the Great Depression, and her own unfulfilled dreams due to a lack of education and an early marriage. Now, when her own daughter announced that she was moving halfway around the world as a missionary, this aging woman lashed out: "If you leave me, then you obviously don't love me! If you don't care enough for me to stay by me as I grow old, then we don't have a relationship. I can't believe my own daughter is doing this to me!"

My grandmother's words and attitude wounded and worried my mother. The fact is that she loved her mother and was devoted to her. But she was also committed to following Christ.

As a six-year-old I remember the final week before we left our home in South Carolina for the Philippines. My family had a huge yard sale. We sold nearly all our furniture and possessions. I particularly remember my mother giving away her childhood dolls, which she had cherished for years, to the little girls that lived next door. Those things had to be left behind.

Saying farewell to cherished friends was even more difficult. And then we made the trip to my grandmother's house to say good-bye. It was not a pretty scene. My mother did not receive her mother's blessing or fond release to embrace her future. There was an icy chill in the air. Mom left more than I can realize to follow the call of Jesus.

But the amazing thing is that in the process, my family received far more than we ever left behind. Soon the missionaries with whom we worked became like uncles and aunts to me. Some of the older missionaries became my grandparents. My mother and father embraced their calling to teach seminary students, and found deep reward in doing so. The house we moved into was simple but comfortable. God not only supplied our needs but also gave to us a feeling of joyful abundance. And perhaps the most amazing thing was that given time, my grandmother slowly had a change of heart. She never told my mother that she was proud of her. But she sure told all of her neighbors that she was. And when my grandmother contracted cancer years later, my mother returned from the Philippines to live with her during the last year of her life, faithful to her relationship as a daughter.

My family discovered—as all maturing Christians discover—that "you can't out-give God!" We learned that what you give away and leave behind is replenished in abundance. We came to understand that if you release your tight grip on personal happiness, you are soon embraced by a deeper level of satisfaction than you have ever known.

Wise men and women have been saying for centuries that when we make finding happiness the major goal of life, we will never be happy. Happiness is not a goal to be discovered, achieved, or obtained. Rather, happiness is the by-product of a life well lived. Happiness is what happens in the process of following Jesus.

What Jesus teaches all his disciples is that the Christian life is full of rich paradox: *When you lose your life, you find it; when you abandon the priority of personal happiness, you become joyful; when you give away your meager lunch to feed the multitude, your gift is multiplied; and when you cease to seek reward, you are most richly blessed.*

Each of us will come to the moment—many moments—when we secretly ask, "What's in it for me, Jesus?" And when we hear our own voice say these words, we teeter on the brink of discovery. If we continue to follow Jesus into the unknown, we will soon discover, with Peter, the depth of true reward.

Reflections

Psalm 37:1; Proverbs 21:21; Matthew 6:33, 25:34-36; 1 Corinthians 2:9; Galatians 6:9

In vain do they talk of happiness who never subdued an impulse in obedience to a principle. He who never sacrificed a present to a future good, or a personal to a general one, can speak of happiness only as the blind speak of colors.
    —*Horace Mann*[3]

I find my joy of living in the fierce and ruthless battles of life, and my pleasure comes from learning something.
    —*August Strindberg*[4]

Happiness does not lie in happiness, but in the achievement of it.
    —*Fyodor Dostoevsky*[5]

To give and not to count the cost;
To fight and not to heed the wounds;
To toil and not to seek for rest;
To labour and not ask for any reward
Save that of knowing that we do Thy will.
   —*St. Ignatius Loyola*[6]

It is not denying oneself fulfillment, but giving up depending on oneself to attain it.
   —*Paul Tournier*[7]

Dear Lord,

I must confess that under a thin veneer of practiced goodness, I often clinch my fists, narrow my eyes, and silently demand to know what my reward will be. I, with the Psalmist, rail against heaven that the rich get richer and the poor get poorer and that it is the selfish who inherit the earth. Sometimes I want to abandon the quest to follow you, and retreat to my home by the lakeside. I want to go fishing again and mind my own business. I long to seek my own reward, to establish my own independence, to control my world.

But God, I am slowly learning that the only way to keep a firm grip on my life is to let go of my life. I must trust you and you alone to guide me to green pastures, to lead me to still waters, to restore my soul. Only you, O Lord, can make me happy. Give me the courage to follow you. Amen.

Questions among Friends

1. Would you be a Christian if you had no promise of eternal life? Why or why not?

2. How has the natural desire to seek personal reward created spiritual struggle for you?

3. Describe a time in your life when you had to give up something that you longed for in order to follow Jesus.

4. What are some of the greatest rewards you have experienced in your years of following Jesus? What has caused you to experience happiness?

Chapter Nine

"HOW OFTEN MUST I FORGIVE MY BROTHER?"

Then Peter came and said to Him, "Lord, how often shall my brother sin against me and I forgive him? Up to seven times?" Jesus said to him, "I do not say to you, up to seven times, but up to seventy times seven.

"For this reason the kingdom of heaven may be compared to a king who wished to settle accounts with his slaves. When he had begun to settle them, one who owed him ten thousand talents was brought to him. But since he did not have the means to repay, his lord commanded him to be sold, along with his wife and children and all that he had, and repayment to be made. So the slave fell to the ground and prostrated himself before him, saying, 'Have patience with me and I will repay you everything.' And the lord of that slave felt compassion and released him and forgave him the debt. But that slave went out and found one of his fellow slaves who owed him a hundred denarii; and he seized him and began to choke him, saying, 'Pay back what you owe.' So his fellow slave fell to the ground and began to plead with him, saying, 'Have patience with me and I will repay you.' But he was unwilling and went and threw him in prison until he should pay back what was owed. So when his fellow-slaves saw what had happened, they were deeply grieved and came and reported to their lord all that had happened. Then summoning him, his lord said to him, 'You wicked slave, I forgave you all that debt because you pleaded with me. Should you not also have had mercy on your fellow slave, in the same way as I had mercy on you?' And his lord, moved with anger, handed him over to the torturers until he should repay all that was owed him. My heavenly Father will also do the same to you, if each of you does not forgive his brother from your heart." (Matthew 18:21-35 [Luke 17:3-4])

AS JESUS AND HIS DISCIPLES RETURNED FROM THEIR RETREAT IN THE cool, mountainous region of northern Israel, they were surrounded again by the heat of tension and pressing danger. From the insight gained on the Mount of Transfiguration, Jesus knew that it was now time to travel to Jerusalem and confront religious and government leaders. He also realized that this encounter would cost him his life.

Perhaps the twelve disciples were not as aware as Jesus was of what lay ahead. But they could feel the tension mounting. Tempers grew short, and patience disappeared. In the midst of this cauldron, somebody pushed Peter one too many times. Growing angry, Peter snapped at Jesus: "Lord, how many times do I have to keep forgiving this jerk? Up to seven times?" Staring into this intense and livid fisherman's face, Jesus realized that a teachable moment had arrived. It was time to talk about forgiveness and discipleship.

Unlimited Forgiveness

Peter had a reason for suggesting that he was willing to forgive his irascible friend up to seven times. Peter probably knew that the Pharisees had deduced that it was necessary to forgive someone who had wronged you up to four times. Later, the Talmud stated that a good Jew should be willing to forgive up to three times. With this in mind, a magnanimous Simon Peter informed Jesus that he was willing to double the Jewish legal requirement for forgiveness. Out of the goodness of his heart, he would consent to walk the second mile. But Peter was also angrily intimating that there must be a reasonable limit to forgiveness.[1]

Much to his surprise, Jesus shot back, "I do not say to you, up to seven times, but up to seventy times seven." In an emphatic way, Jesus insisted that in the kingdom of God, forgiveness has no limits. As God is always ready to forgive, so must God's children forgive.

To illustrate his point, Jesus told a parable that is recorded only in the Gospel of Matthew, the parable of the unmerciful slave. In this preposterous and intentionally exaggerated story, a servant—probably a business manager—has pocketed ten thousand talents of his master's money. With a twinkle in his eye, Jesus knew that he was pushing the limits of Peter's credibility, because ten thousand talents was ten times the total annual revenue of King Herod's kingdom—an incredible sum! Yet despite this unimaginable debt, the dishonest servant was forgiven by his master. As soon as the scoundrel was pardoned, though, he encountered one of his fellow slaves, grabbed him by the throat, and threw him into debtor's prison because he owed him the small sum of one talent—the equivalent of a common laborer's daily wage.[2]

Jesus' point is clear: God's forgiveness is unlimited—preposterously unlimited—and so our forgiveness must be without end. Although forgiveness can be doled out and measured in the world, forgiveness should be of unlimited quantity among Christians.

Jesus' teaching hit me forcefully not long ago. I have rarely been offended or attacked by a friend. But at some time over the course of life, this usually happens to us all. I guess it was my turn, and I was blindsided by a friend's disloyalty. Picking myself up off the ground, I wanted to strike out in anger and get even. I was hurt and angry, and there was no way to disguise or suppress my feelings. Rage and indignity saturated me.

It so happened that, several weeks later, I discovered that forgiveness was my sermon topic for the next Sunday. I recoiled at the task of even thinking about forgiveness. In fact, I seriously considered deviating from my sermon plan and choosing another topic. I was frozen by indecision and a bitter, intransigent heart.

Late one night as I sat stewing at my desk, I happened to read a quotation by C. S. Lewis: "To be a Christian means to forgive the inexcusable, because God has forgiven the inexcusable in you." Lewis's words flew off the page and slapped me in the face. I knew exactly what the old bard meant.[3]

Many times I have sinned against God in inexcusable ways. I have been flagrantly disloyal, selfish in my decisions, and incredibly unwilling to change some of my sinful and destructive ways. Again and again, I have asked God to forgive me. And because God is God, I do believe that I have been faithfully pardoned for my transgressions.

Yet, that night as I reflected on C. S. Lewis's words and considered my friend's vicious actions toward me, my fists knotted up and my eyes narrowed into vengeful slits. I wanted to emotionally draw and quarter the rascal and spit on his grave. "What he did was inexcusable! Absolutely inexcusable!" I bellowed. And that was when C. S. Lewis's well-honed words convicted me.

Yes, what my friend did was inexcusable. But that doesn't mean that I cannot forgive him. For if inexcusable actions are truly unpardonable, then we are all—to use my grandfather's words—going to hell in a handbasket!

Now, let's be clear and honest. Jesus doesn't say that we should not learn important lessons from people who hurt us. Jesus doesn't ask us to become emotional punching bags for every bully who walks into our life. Jesus doesn't say that we shouldn't carefully choose whom we can and cannot trust. But Jesus does say that we must always be ready to forgive, release our anger and hatred, bury the offense, and get on with life.

Not to forgive is to retain a terrible poison in the psyche, one that is toxic to spiritual and physical health. To forgive—truly forgive—purges us of such poison so we may enter a fresh new chapter of life. Forgiveness is a spiritual necessity for all who would follow Jesus.

Forgiveness: The Symbol of Christianity

Forgiveness is also the outward symbol of Christianity to our world. Where forgiveness is not displayed and exemplified by Christians, the integrity and the power of the Gospel is diluted and distorted.

Recently I was reading an account of Christopher Columbus's discovery of the so-called New World. As Columbus approached the uncharted isles of the Caribbean, the canvas sails of his three small caravels prominently displayed the cross of Christ, the symbol of Christianity and the chosen emblem of the Spanish fleet. As the European ships sailed above the horizon, the first image glimpsed by uncomprehending native Caribs was the blood-red symbol of Christianity—a cross—the sign of God's sacrificial forgiveness of humankind.

Upon encountering the native "Indians," Columbus found them to be friendly and hospitable. He wrote in his *diario,* or logbook, "In all the world there can be no better or gentler people." Knowing that Queen Isabella would one day read his *diario,* the religious Columbus went on to implore, "I maintain, Most Serene Princes, that if [the Indians] had access to devout religious persons knowing the language, they would all turn Christian, and so I hope in Our Lord that Your Highnesses will do something about it with much care, in order to turn to the Church so numerous a folk."

Within days, however, Spanish Christians were treating these "gentle people" with a ruthless and unforgiving viciousness that undercut any positive Christian witness. On landing on La Isabella, Columbus sent a foraging party to the interior to find food. While fording a river, some of the natives accompanying Columbus's sailors took some of the European clothing the sailors had cast aside. Later, when one of the Indian men was found wearing the clothing, he was seized and accused of theft. To set an example as to what would happen to people who broke Spanish law, the man was trussed up and his ears cut off. Bartolomé de Las Casas, a Dominican friar who knew Columbus and preserved portions of his now lost logbook, wrote of this violent incident: "This was the first injustice, with vain and erroneous pretension of doing justice, that was committed in these Indies against the Indians, and the beginning of the shedding of blood which has since flowed so copiously."[4]

As I read this tragic account, the wrenching irony of what took place hit me. Columbus had wanted the Caribs to hear in their own language the gospel of Jesus Christ. Yet, because of Christians who would not love and forgive, the very ears of those who could have heard the gospel had been sliced off by swords, and the Spirit of Christ had been defamed.

When Christians are not seen as people who are quick to forgive, the credibility of the Christian faith is compromised, if not destroyed. Large red crosses prominently displayed on our canvas sails do not convince anyone that we are Christians. But an attitude of perpetual forgiveness never fails to convict others of the truth of Christ.

❧

As Jesus approached Jerusalem, he knew that he must teach his disciples by word and example that the ability to forgive without limits is at the heart of the Gospel. The simple fact is that if you follow Jesus, you will be crucified many times by thoughtless people whose actions are "inexcusable." Yet—as Jesus would soon show Peter—we must learn to whisper from our cross of misunderstanding, "Father, forgive them, for they know not what they do."

Reflections

Psalm 103:8-14, Psalm 130:3-4, Matthew 6:12, Mark 11:25, Luke 6:37, Ephesians 4:31-32

We must be clear about one thing regarding forgiveness. Forgiveness is not so much the remission of penalty as the restoration of a relationship.
—*William Barclay*[5]

Leonardo da Vinci began painting his famous painting, *The Last Supper,* in a time of anger against a fellow artist whom he painted as Judas. Finally, unable to paint the face of Jesus, he erased the vengeful portrait and replaced it with another. Thus he was able to complete the face of Christ. We cannot paint God's forgiveness into our lives while holding bitter spite for others.
—*The Quarterly Review*[6]

It is easier to forgive an enemy than to forgive a friend.
—*William Blake*[7]

Dear Lord,
It is hard not to grow fixated on anger, to clutch my wounds and savor my lust for revenge. There is toxic sweetness to a grudge carefully kept. And warm is the ember of hatred tended and stoked each new morning. I must admit, oh God, that I am quite unforgiving.
Lord, save me from myself. Release the bitterness from my soul. And may I not in a spirit of self-righteousness sever the ears of those who yearn to hear the gracious tones of your gospel.
Enable my forgiveness to have no end. Amen.

Questions among Friends

1. Share with your friends a time when you experienced a spirit of unforgiveness that hurt a friendship, a family, a church, or a nation.

2. Can you relate a time when you had difficulty forgiving someone?

3. Discuss how you might forgive a person for hurting you, yet at the same time, learn to protect yourself from physical, emotional, or spiritual abuse.

4. Discuss this statement made by the nineteenth-century American Congregationalist pastor Henry Ward Beecher: "*I can forgive, but I cannot forget!' is only another way of saying, 'I cannot forgive.'*"[8]

Chapter Ten

SERVANTS TO ONE ANOTHER

When the hour had come, He reclined at the table, and the apostles with Him. And He said to them, "I have earnestly desired to eat this Passover with you before I suffer; for I say to you, I shall never again eat it until it is fulfilled in the kingdom of God. . . ."

And there arose also a dispute among them as to which one of them was regarded to be greatest. And He said to them, "The kings of the Gentiles lord it over them; and those who have authority over them are called 'Benefactors.' But it is not this way with you, but the one who is the greatest among you must become like the youngest, and the leader like the servant. For who is greater, the one who reclines at the table, or the one who serves? Is it not the one who reclines at the table? But I am among you as the one who serves." (Luke 22:14-16, 24-26)

Now before the feast of the Passover, Jesus knowing that His hour had come that He would depart out of this world to the Father, having loved His own who were in the world, He loved them to the end. During supper, the devil having already put into the heart of Judas Iscariot, the son of Simon, to betray Him, Jesus, knowing that the Father had given all things into His hands, and that He had come forth from God and was going back to God, got up from supper, and laid aside His garments; and taking a towel, He girded Himself. Then He poured water into the basin, and began to wash the disciples' feet and to wipe them with the towel with which He was girded. So He came to Simon Peter. He said to Him, "Lord, do You wash my feet?" Jesus answered and said to him, "What I do you do not realize now; but you will understand hereafter." Peter said to Him, "Never shall You wash my feet!" Jesus answered him, "If I do not wash you, you have no part with Me." Simon Peter said to Him, "Lord, then wash not only my feet, but also my hands and my head." Jesus said to him, "He who has bathed needs only to wash his feet, but is completely clean; and you are clean, but not all of you." For He knew the one who was betraying Him; for this reason He said, "Not all of you are clean."

So when He had washed their feet, and taken His garments and reclined at the table again, He said to them, "Do you know what I have done to you? You call Me Teacher and Lord; and you are right; for so I am. If I then, the Lord and the Teacher, washed your feet, you also ought to wash one another's feet. For I gave you an example that you also should do as I did to you." (John 13:1-15)

JESUS SENSED THAT THE TRIGGER EVENT LEADING TO HIS DEATH would be his observance of Passover in Jerusalem. Every Jewish male throughout the Mediterranean world would attempt, if possible, to make a pilgrimage to Jerusalem for Passover. As the seven-day festival approached, the population of Jerusalem would swell fivefold, from approximately forty thousand to nearly two hundred thousand people.[1] Surrounded by this throng of Jewish pilgrims who were inflamed with nationalistic spirit, the Roman army occupying Jerusalem would be on high alert. Expecting uprising and revolution at any moment, the troops of Caesar would have no patience and extend little mercy. Jerusalem was a powder keg awaiting the spark of controversy to explode. And Jesus was controversial.

As the fresh, golden ears of barley ripened in the Judean fields in late March, Jesus and his disciples slowly began to wind their way toward Jerusalem. Before they would eat their Passover meal together in Jerusalem, several conflictive events would transpire, which would escalate the tension between Jesus and the Jewish religious leaders.

First, Jesus had made it his custom to stay with friends in Bethany when visiting Jerusalem on feast days. Bethany was a small village lying on the lower slope of an eastern ridge of the Mount of Olives, two miles east of Jerusalem. Jesus' close friend, Lazarus, lived with his sisters, Mary and Martha, in Bethany. While traveling to visit them, Jesus received word that Lazarus had suddenly died. When Jesus arrived four days after the death, he was overcome with grief and performed the greatest miracle of his ministry. Standing before the tomb of Lazarus, he commanded that the power of God resuscitate Lazarus's body, that the physical process of decay disappear, and that Lazarus walk from the grave alive and whole. Lazarus stumbled forth from the grave, still draped in burial wrappings.

A miracle of this magnitude could not be suppressed. The chief priests and the scribes immediately convened an emergency council and declared; "What are we doing? For this man is performing many signs. If we let Him go on like this, all men will believe in Him, and the Romans will come and take away both our place and our nation." They concluded their meeting with the decision that Jesus must immediately be brought to trial and executed (John 11:1-57).

Following the resuscitation of Lazarus, Jesus left Bethany to visit Jerusalem. Expecting to see more miracles, Jews from Bethany accompanied him and staged a demonstration as he neared one of the Jerusalem gates. Waving palm branches and throwing their cloaks down before him, they created a scene worthy of a returning conqueror. By their words and actions, they declared that they believed Jesus was the Messiah (John 12:12-19).

It is likely that this was a small demonstration, perhaps barely noticed amid the thousands of Jews crowding into Jerusalem. But to the eyes of the Sanhedrin spies who now followed Jesus' every move, the symbolic palm branches waved by the little crowd added more fuel to the fire.

Then came the most dangerous action. Entering the Temple in Jerusalem, Jesus followed the tradition of the ancient prophets and performed a public protest that could have been disastrous for the Jews. Incensed by the flagrant profiteering taking place in the Court of the Gentiles by merchants who sold animals for sacrifice, as well as vendors who exchanged foreign money for Jewish currency, Jesus erupted in anger and began to overturn the merchants' tables. Wielding a whip, he shouted, "My house shall be called a house of prayer for all the nations. But you have made it a robbers' den." (Mark 11:17).[2]

At the very moment Jesus was creating this furor, hundreds of Roman soldiers were only a stone's throw away. The Romans anticipated that if the Jews ever revolted against Rome, the revolution would start on the Temple grounds. Therefore they had converted the Fortress Antonia, an old Hasmonean castle connected to the northwest corner of the Temple, into quarters for a Roman cohort. With the least provocation, Roman soldiers could charge directly down a flight of stairs and into the Temple grounds to crush any demonstration. Jesus' visceral confrontation with the Temple merchants could have caused a massacre.[3]

But this did not happen. Jesus made his prophetic protest, disappeared into the crowd, and a crisis was averted. But Jesus had sealed his fate. A public demonstration in the Temple was ample grounds for formal charges of insurrection and the foment of revolution. The Jewish rulers now had adequate evidence to arrest Jesus and bring him before the Roman tribunal on the grounds of insurrection against Rome, a capital offense by Roman law.

After sunset on Passover eve—the first day of Unleavened Bread—Jesus and his disciples again slipped back into the walls of Jerusalem and met for their Passover meal in an upstairs banquet room of a private home.[4] Earlier in the day, Peter and John had made preparations for the meal, and now thirteen men were reclined in Roman fashion around a festive table of simple food.[5] As Jesus gazed at the strained faces of the disciples who had followed him for months, he winced, knowing that Judas was no longer loyal to him. In fact, he was aware that in recent days this man had conspired with the Jewish leaders to trap and arrest him. Only hours, if not minutes, now separated Jesus from a violent fate.

As small talk ensued around the room, only the Gospel of Luke gives insight into the disciples' conversation. Luke states, "And there arose also a dispute among them as to which one of them was regarded to be greatest" (Luke 22:24). This quest for power and advantage seemed to be a common rankling theme among Jesus' disciples. Still convinced that Jesus would somehow wrench political victory from the jaws of defeat, they fiercely jockeyed for position. Their game of one-upmanship had always been intense. And Jesus knew that this seismic flaw in their fellowship was far more dangerous than the opposition of the Jewish Sanhedrin or the might of Rome.

Perhaps above the ferment of intense whispers, it was the smell of stinking feet that jarred Jesus into action. Devout Jews were a clean and fastidious people. Before a special banquet feast, they would often bathe and anoint their bodies with perfume. Then, after walking in sandals on dusty paths to the home of their host, they would be greeted at the door with pitchers of water to pour over their dirty feet. No such civility had greeted Jesus that night.

Etiquette aside, Jews were peculiar about their feet. Hygienic though they might be, Jewish Law stated that not even a slave could be forced to wash his or her master's feet. Feet were private and intimate parts of the body, and such coerced action was perceived as obscene. When done voluntarily, however, the washing of another person's feet was seen as a symbol of love and devotion, a sign of deep and abiding friendship. Often, the disciples of a respected rabbi would wash their master's feet before he taught them. But no one on this Passover night had paused to wash even their own feet.[6]

Perhaps inspired by this observation, Jesus suddenly stood in the midst of his bickering disciples and filled a basin with water. Then he did what any slave would do who was to engage in dirty labor. He took off his outer cloak and inner tunic so as not to stain them. He wrapped himself simply with what the writer of the Gospel of John calls a towel, and proceeded to work. Garbed as a simple servant, Jesus washed his disciples' feet. The irony of his actions was lost on no one. Here the honored rabbi—the beloved teacher— was reversing protocol and washing the feet of his disciples. The effect was sobering and powerful.

When Jesus knelt to wash Simon Peter's feet, Peter recoiled. Powerful symbol or not, Peter could not bear the thought of Jesus stooping to wash his soiled feet. Peter insisted, "Never shall You wash my feet!" Jesus answered him, "If I do not wash you, you have no part with Me. Peter then impulsively blurted out, "Lord, then wash not only my feet, but also my hands and my head" (John 13:8).

Finished with his act of teaching, Jesus wanted to make sure that the disciples understood the symbol enacted before them. He said, "Do you know what I have done to you? You call me Teacher and Lord; and you are right, for so I am. If I then, the Lord and the Teacher, washed your feet, you also ought to wash one another's feet. For I gave you an example that you also should do as I have done to you. Truly, truly, I say to you, a slave is not greater than his master; nor is one who is sent greater than the one who sent him. If you know these things, you are blessed if you do them" (John 13:12-17).

A Willingness to Be a Servant

If Jesus had demonstrated nothing else in the last few days, he had amply shown his courage and raw bravery. It took a daring and resolute man to stage a demonstration in the Temple, under the nose of a Roman garrison. Jesus was no meek and mild spiritualist. He was a true son of David, who would attack a giant with a slingshot.

But it was exactly this grit and tenacity that made his spontaneous act of washing the disciples' feet so poignant. Here was a strong, sinewy carpenter kneeling before his own friends and quietly washing the road dust from their feet. The disciples could recall countless times when Jesus had said that being a servant to others was central to being a child of God. But now they had seen the meaning of servanthood memorialized forever.

Some sixty years later, when the writers of the Gospels of Mark, Matthew, and Luke had already written their Gospels, the future author of the Gospel of John likely noted that they had not included the story of the foot washing. Thus, when John later penned his account of the Last Supper, the foot washing became his central motif. So moved was he by this moment that he could not let it slip into the silent oblivion of unspoken history. Rather, he was impelled to tell the story of when the Son of God did what a slave could not be forced to do, and washed away the grime of life's journey from tired and worn feet. John saw this Passover night scene as fitting prelude to the event of the very next day, when Jesus was tortured, tried, and crucified. Against the specter of the cross, John saw the greatest symbol of servanthood—when the blood of Christ and the tears of God spiritually washed away the sins of the world.

Reflecting on these same images in a different time and place, the Apostle Paul wrote to Christians at Philippi who were feuding with one another, and quoted to them the words of the most ancient Christian liturgy preserved:

Have this attitude in yourselves which was also in Christ Jesus, who, although He existed in the form of God, did not regard equality with God

a thing to be grasped, but emptied Himself, taking the form of a bond-ser-
vant, and being made in the likeness of men. Being found in appearance as
a man, He humbled Himself by becoming obedient to the point of death,
even death on a cross. For this reason also, God highly exalted Him, and
bestowed on Him the name which is above every name, so that at the name
of Jesus every knee will bow, of those who are in heaven and on earth and
under the earth, and that every tongue will confess that Jesus Christ is
Lord, to the glory of God the Father." (Philippians 2:5-11)

On a night long ago, Simon Peter, John, and their fellow disciples
learned that greatness in the kingdom of God does not come through
achievement, power, or fame. Greatness comes through loving others in a
way that no human law could ever coerce. Godly love is known when we
touch the dirt in one another's lives—the road dust of the years—and ten-
derly wash it away.

A Willingness to Accept Love

Perhaps the greatest lesson of this Passover night, however, is an insight that
is frequently overlooked. For Simon Peter the climactic moment came when
he cowered behind his own fear of intimacy and his pride, and refused to let
Jesus wash his feet. Jesus reprimanded him, and told him, "If I do not wash
you, you have no part with Me." Peter had to learn a difficult lesson—that
for Christians love must be *as freely received as it is given.*

As I write these words, it is Christmastime. I have just returned from visiting with a young, single mother, Anna, who is having a difficult time. Anna
is by nature a caring woman. She has been active in many ministries through
our church, including helping to prepare meals for elderly people who are
homebound. Several years ago, Anna went through a painful divorce and was
awarded custody of her three young children. More recently she lost her job
when the industry in which she worked relocated to another state, and her
former husband is behind in his support payments.

Late this afternoon I dropped by to see Anna. I knew that she did not
have money for Christmas presents this year, and I wanted to give her some
money from our church to help her and her children. As we talked I told her
how much the people of our church cared for her, and that we wanted to
walk with her during this painful period of her life. As I prepared to leave, I
reached out to hand her the check in an envelope. With tears running down
her cheeks, Anna put her hands in her pockets, looked down at her feet, and
shook her head. "No," she said, "I can't take it. There are people who need it
worse than I do."

"I know there are people who may need it more than you do, Anna," I replied, "but you are missing the point. The point is that you are part of a church family that loves you. Please let us share the joy of helping one another."

As Anna stood perplexed and undecided, I told her of a time, shortly after Beth and I were married, when I was completely broke. Five days after our wedding, we moved from Georgia to Louisville, Kentucky, where I was to enter seminary. Three months after our move, neither Beth nor I had been able to find a job. The economy was in recession, and I was down to my last five dollars.

One day after my final class, I trudged to the financial aid office like a man walking to the gallows. I nervously asked to speak with Dr. Norman Shands, a kind, elderly minister who helped students work through their financial problems. When Dr. Shands asked me about my own situation, I sat there blushing, wordless, and looking at my feet, much like Anna. Finally I mumbled: "For the first time in my life, Dr. Shands, I'm broke. And I don't have family to turn to. I just don't know what to do."

While he listened to me ramble, Dr. Shands took out his fountain pen and began to scribble in a checkbook. When I finally ran out of words, he tore the check from the book and handed it to me. The amount was five hundred dollars. I sat there stunned and confused and profoundly grateful.

Quietly Dr. Shands told me that the seminary had a fund that had been contributed to by alumni and friends for more than one hundred years. The fund was to help struggling students get their feet on the ground. The five hundred dollars was a loan, he said. However, if I was still in the ministry five years after graduation, then the loan was cancelled and did not need to be remitted.

As I drove home that night, check in my shirt pocket, I thought about the nameless Christians who loved me and were supporting me in my studies. And now, twenty-eight years later, I am still in the ministry and still nourished by their love.

As I was telling this story to Anna, I could see her relax. With a shy smile on her face, she accepted the check. She was learning that to be children of God, we must be able to receive love as well as give love.

To be an able servant in God's kingdom, we must always keep a balance between giving and receiving love. We must remember that shortly before his death, Jesus allowed Mary, the sister of Lazarus, to pour costly perfume on his feet and wipe away the road dust with her hair. It was such a lavish display of love that some called it foolish and were offended. But Jesus knew that he needed to receive love too. And if Jesus needed to accept the demonstrated love of others, then so do we (John 12:1-8).

Reflections
Mark 10:42-45, Luke 22:27, Romans 12:10, Galatians 5:13

Example is not the main thing in influencing others. It is the only thing.
—*Albert Schweitzer*[7]

God has given us two hands—one for receiving and the other for giving.
—*Billy Graham*[8]

Not he who has much is free, but he who gives much.
—*Erich Fromm*[9]

Should not the given be thankful that the receiver received? Is not giving a need? Is not receiving mercy?
—*Friedrich Nietzsche*[10]

A hundred times every day I remind myself that my inner and outer life are based on the labors of other men, living and dead, and that I must exert myself in order to give in the same measure as I have received and am still receiving.
—*Albert Einstein*[11]

Dear Father,

It is often hard for me to receive the love of others. When someone seeks to wash my feet by giving me a warm compliment or extending praise, I often blush, bow my head, and make light of their affirmation. My own insecurity—my awkward need for love—prohibits me from entering into their warm embrace. With Peter, I draw back and murmur, "Never shall You wash my feet!"

But Lord, if I do not allow others to tame me—permit their hands to touch my feet and warm my heart—then I shall never be happy. For what is life but misery without the gentle, healing touch of friendship?

Give me the courage to accept intimacy. May I allow my road-weary feet to be soothed and bathed by others. May the waters of their friendship heal the cuts and ease the pain of life's bruises. And may their love enable me to abandon the petty competitions of this world and kneel to serve others. Amen.

Questions among Friends

1. Describe a time in your life when somebody "washed your feet" by loving you, accepting you, or encouraging you. Has their example helped you to wash the feet of others?

2. Is it easier for you to give love or to receive love?

3. Like the disciples, do you have a tendency to be competitive with your friends? Has this interfered with your friendships? How have you learned to handle this aspect of your personality?

4. Discuss some practical ways you can "wash the feet" of others.

Chapter Eleven

"THE SPIRIT IS WILLING, BUT THE FLESH IS WEAK"

And after singing a hymn, they went out to the Mount of Olives.

And Jesus said to them, "You will all fall away, because it is written, 'I will strike down the shepherd, and the sheep shall be scattered.' But after I have been raised, I will go ahead of you to Galilee. But Peter said to Him, "Even though all may fall away, yet I will not." And Jesus said to him, "Truly I say to you, that this very night, before a rooster crows twice, you yourself will deny Me three times." But Peter kept saying insistently, "Even if I have to die with You, I will not deny You!" And they all were saying the same thing also.

They came to a place named Gethsemane; and He said to His disciples, "Sit here until I have prayed." And He took with Him Peter and James and John, and began to be very distressed and troubled. And He said to them, "My soul is deeply grieved to the point of death; remain here and keep watch." And He went a little beyond them, and fell to the ground and began to pray that if it were possible, the hour might pass Him by. And He was saying, "Abba! Father! All things are possible for You; remove this cup from Me; yet not what I will, but what You will." And He came and found them sleeping, and said to Peter, "Simon, are you asleep? Could you not keep watch for one hour? Keep watching and praying, that you may not come into temptation; the spirit is willing, but the flesh is weak." And again He went away and prayed, saying the same words. And again He came and found them sleeping, for their eyes were very heavy; and they did not know what to answer Him. And he came the third time, and said to them, "Are you still sleeping and resting? It is enough; the hour has come; behold, the Son of Man is being betrayed into the hands of sinners. Get up, let us be going; behold, the one who betrays Me is at hand!" (Mark 14:26-42)

[Jesus] went forth with His disciples over the ravine of the Kidron, where there was a garden, in which He entered with His disciples. Now Judas also, who was betraying Him, knew the place, for Jesus had often met there with His disciples. Judas then, having received the Roman cohort and officers from the chief priests and the Pharisees, came there with lanterns and torches and weapons. . . . Simon Peter then, having a sword, drew it and struck the high priest's slave, and cut off his right ear; and the slave's name was Malchus. So Jesus said to Peter, "Put the sword into the sheath; the cup which the Father has given Me, shall I not drink it?" (John 18:1-3, 10-12)

As John Mark wrote his Gospel in Rome, in the midst of the bloody carnage of Nero's persecution of Christians, he knew that his readers would easily relate to the suffering of Jesus and the fear of his disciples. He therefore brought the character of Peter to the center of his Gospel stage, and focused the spotlight on him. John Mark's portrait of Peter depicts a follower of Jesus' who is caught in the midst of perplexing times and is ravaged by fear, confusion, weakness, failure, and betrayal. Peter demonstrates the struggle of all Christians as he walks with Jesus toward the climactic moments of his arrest, trial, and crucifixion.

When Jesus and his disciples concluded their Passover meal, they followed tradition and sang the *Great Hallel,* Psalm 136. They then left the upper room, slipped through the guarded gates of Jerusalem, crossed the dark Kidron Valley, and came to the Garden of Gethsemane, on the Mount of Olives. Only the writer of the Gospel of John tells us that Jesus had retreated to this garden "often" with his disciples. It was a familiar place of refuge.

It Can't Happen to Me

En route to Gethsemane, Jesus spoke words of warning that set Peter's teeth on edge. Jesus grimly said, "You will all fall away." Put more bluntly, Jesus predicted that every one of his handpicked disciples would desert him, flee when the going got tough, and cave in to fear and temptation.

Peter was incensed. With steel in his voice, he shot back: "Even though all may fall away, yet I will not. Even if I have to die with You, I will not deny You!" And all the disciples echoed his stubborn allegiance.

As I reflect on these words, I am reminded of many personal interviews I have read of American soldiers who fought in World War II. It seems that most combat troops on the eve of battle or invasion are filled with fear and dread. As they look about them, they can imagine members of their platoon or flight crew—even their best buddies—being mortally wounded, blown to bits, or shrouded in body bags. However, the one thing that most cannot envision is losing their own life. Indeed, on the eve of great danger, the denial factor is so high in all of us that mentally we say, "This can't happen to me!"

The fact is that many of the combat troops at Anzio, Normandy, and Iwo Jima who denied their own mortality met death within hours. And many of them died with looks of horrible surprise on their face. All of us are equally vulnerable to defeat, failure, and death.

Several days ago I was cleaning out a file drawer and came across a twenty-five-year-old picture of my seminary graduation class. I smiled fondly as I looked at the fresh, young faces of my friends from days gone by. It was the eve of graduation, and we were setting out to "win the world for Christ." Little could we have known what lay ahead of us. But the truth is that all these young men and women—myself included—have been assaulted by the evil in this world, have faced fierce temptation, have been battered by disillusionment, and have often failed and betrayed Christ by the way we have lived.

Ironically, it is often the brightest and best who stumble the most. Thomas Fuller (1654-1734), an English clergyman who endured the ravages of the English Civil War, once commented, "Good swimmers are oftenest drowned."[1] Fuller recognized that it is those who are the strongest and most able who are often the ones caught in the undertow and riptides of Satan. Because of their ability and talent, such strong swimmers rise quickly to leadership roles and positions of responsibility. They seem invincible. But quite the opposite is true. Because they are strong swimmers, they are often the ones sent to rescue others in the most treacherous waters. Caught in the crosscurrents of a seductive and violent world, the strong swimmers are often sucked under and swept away by the lure of power, fame, sex, money, and self-worship. It can be dangerous to have the gift of being a strong swimmer.

In writing to Christians who were under persecution in Rome, John Mark emphasized the theme that often it is the strong who must be most on guard. No man or woman is exempt from the power of temptation or the grip of fear. Not even the great Apostle Peter was able to avoid public and humiliating disgrace. Therefore, if we do not recognize our vulnerability, then we have set ourselves up for failure. The mature Christian is one who has come to respect the power of evil and to know that temptation and fear can destroy the best of Christ's disciples.

The Power of Prayer

It has been noted that throughout their long apprenticeship with Jesus, the disciples asked him only once to teach them a specific skill. The writer of Luke states that one day as the disciples observed Jesus' power and ability to minister, they came to him and said, "Lord, teach us to pray." Jesus then taught them what we call the Lord's Prayer (Luke 11:1-4).

Certainly the disciples could have asked Jesus for his trade secrets: "How do you calm a storm? How do you heal a blind man or cast out a demon? How do you feed five thousand people?" However, they correctly perceived that all Jesus' ability came from one central source—his ability to pray and be connected to the power of God the Father. Prayer is the secret—the one and only secret—to the Christian disciple's ability to thwart evil in our universe.

When the disciples finally arrived at the Garden of Gethsemane, Jesus took Peter, James, and John, and withdrew to the interior of the garden to pray. Jesus was emotionally pressed to the breaking point, and he knew it. He had a scant few minutes left to change his mind, to retreat back to Galilee, to fall back on another course of action and avoid arrest and execution. No sane man wants to be tortured and die a violent death—and Jesus didn't either.

One of the beautiful things about the Gospel record is that no attempt was made to portray Jesus as one who did not fear, who never wavered, who was not afraid. Jesus did plead, "My Father, . . . let this cup pass from Me" (Matthew 26:39). He did cry out in agony, "My God, My God, why have You forsaken me?" (Matthew 27:46). Jesus experienced the full spectrum of human emotions. Yet despite his feelings, Jesus was faithful to the end. And he was faithful because he was intimately connected to God through prayer.

I was once in conversation with an alcoholic who had been sober for a number of years. I asked him what was the secret to his recovery. He replied: "Well, as simple as it sounds, it was the hardest lesson for me to learn. Every time I crave a drink, the last thing in the world I want to do is pray. I will do anything not to pray. But I finally discovered that when the pressure builds up to get drunk and go on a binge, if I will force myself to pray for five minutes, the temptation will fade away. But you don't know how hard that is. When a man needs a drink, the last thing he wants to do is pray about it."

So it was with Jesus and the disciples. Jesus withdrew to pray, and asked his closest friends to pray with him. But while Jesus connected himself to the source of God's power, Peter, James, and John fell asleep. Whether they prayed or slept made all the difference when the time of conflict descended on them.

Trusting Our Own Resources

When the hammer finally came down—when Peter awoke to find himself surrounded by the bright, smoking torches of the Temple guard and the Roman soldiers—Peter proved that he was a truly brave man. Against all odds he jumped up and resorted to what little power he had. From under his cloak he pulled a short sword and swung at the enemy closest to him. The unfortunate man he struck was Malchus, the high priest's servant. Malchus lost his right ear. But Peter lost the battle.

From this point on, we do not know what happened to Peter or the rest of the disciples. Most likely they fled for their lives, scattering into the dark night. As they disappeared from the arresting mob, Jesus stood soberly, quietly, in control of the situation, and allowed himself to be arrested. Prayer had enabled Jesus to meet this hour of crisis. Waking from sleep, the disciples merely fled.

It is a fact that when we do not pray, we do not depend on God's resources but rather on our own abilities—and our ability is never enough. Granted, God's ways are not always our ways, and God's resources often seem to be wholly inadequate. Indeed, God's approach to the final defeat of evil can seem to us—to use the words of the Apostle Paul—as absolute "foolishness" (1 Corinthians 1:18-25). But the question we must ask ourselves is this: "Do we want to win the battle for the universe through *God's* ability, or do we want to slice off a poor man's ear with our ability?"

Too often Christians want to marshal only the sources of money, education, fervor, and willpower to usher in the kingdom of God on this earth. One more program, one more missionary agency, one more spiritual leader will do the job. Each generation dreams such dreams. But when the day is over, night has descended, fatigue has taken its toll, and the full power of evil is rampant, the only thing that will usher in God's kingdom is to be connected to God's power through prayer. Our resources are useless without prayer.

Last week I was on a mission trip, working in an orphanage in the high, remote mountains of Guatemala. The orphanage was primitive and had many needs. The orphans had no mattresses to sleep on. They were in dire need.

Pooling our money, our mission team found and purchased twenty new bunk beds and mattresses. This would provide comfortable sleeping for all the children in the orphanage. There was one problem, however. The bunk beds had to be rounded up from many different stores across Guatemala, collected in a central place, and then trucked up mountainous roads. On the day before we were to leave, I became discouraged. It was obvious that the bunks would not arrive before our mission team's departure. Indeed, I knew that the beds might not ever be delivered. So I began to do the one thing that I often turn to as a last resort. I began to pray.

As the sun set, I watched the orphans eat their meager supper and prepare for another night of sleep. I felt defeated. And then I heard the blare of a truck's air horn at the orphanage gate. The bunk beds and mattresses had arrived. When my resources and hope had been depleted, the power of prayer came through.

Of course, things did not work out so neatly for Jesus. Despite his most fervent prayer, arrest was not avoided. He was not spared torture or death. But on resurrection morning, the power of God came through. Victory was snatched from the jaws of defeat, and the power of prayer and the faithfulness of God were revealed for all time.

For every Christian, a time will come when all our resources fail us. We will be left with no other help but prayer. And even if death itself should take us, we will discover that God has answered our prayer.

FOR THE BATTERED AND BLOODIED CHRISTIANS IN ROME, PRAYER was an important word to hear and to see, dramatized in the life of Peter. The strongest swimmers do grow weary and falter, but the buoyancy of prayer can save us. Our resources do become depleted, but God's resources are inexhaustible. Every Christian will experience nights of agony and defeat, when we are arrested and manacled by the powers of this world. But for those who follow Christ, there will always be the rising sun of resurrection morning.

Reflections
1 Corinthians 10:12-13, Philippians 4:6-7

Danger breeds best on too much confidence.
   —*Thomas Corneille*[2]

She understood the nature of sin and knew that its most volatile form was the kind that did not recognize itself.
   —*Pat Conroy*[3]

At times our strengths propel us so far forward we can no longer endure our weaknesses and perish from them.
   —*Friedrich Nietzsche*[4]

A solitary shriek, the bubbling cry, of some strong swimmer in his agony.
   —*Lord Byron*[5]

When the conflicting currents of the unconscious create engulfing whirlpools, the waters can again be guided into a single current if the dam sluice be opened into the channel of prayer—and if that channel has been dug deep enough.
   —*Dag Hammarskjöld*[6]

Prayer is not instinctive like eating. I wish it were, and that one really hungered for God. If I give up food, I am driven to eat; the less I eat the more I want to, but the less I pray the less I want to.
—Leslie D. Weatherhead[7]

One way to recollect the mind easily in the time of prayer and preserve it more in tranquility, is not to let it wander too far at other times. You should keep it strictly in the presence of God; and being accustomed to think of Him often you will find it easy to keep your mind calm in the time of prayer, or at best to recall it from its wanderings.
—Brother Lawrence[8]

If you slip and stumble and forget God for an hour, and assert your old proud self, and rely upon your own clever wisdom, don't spend too much time in anguished regrets and self-accusations but begin again, just where you are.
—Thomas R. Kelly[9]

Dear Father,

I must confess that in my times of trial and crisis, I turn to my own inner strength for help. And when I do, I usually fail. Help me to learn to depend upon your strength and not my own. Teach me to pray and to be connected to your presence. May I not fall asleep when you ask me to keep watch and to pray. Amen.

Questions among Friends

1. Can you think of a time when you thought you were a strong swimmer but the current of life proved too treacherous for you to fight against?

2. Do you recall an event or occasion when you said, "This can't happen to me!" but it did?

3. What things make it most difficult for you to pray?

4. In what ways do you personally identify with Peter in this story?

5. What is the most important thing you have learned from reflecting on Peter's experience in the Garden of Gethsemane?

Chapter Twelve

"I DO NOT KNOW
THIS MAN!"

They led Jesus away to the high priest; and all the chief priests and the elders and the scribes gathered together. Peter had followed Him at a distance, right into the courtyard of the high priest; and he was sitting with the officers and warming himself at the fire. . . .

As Peter was below in the courtyard, one of the servant-girls of the high priest came, and seeing Peter warming himself, she looked at him and said, "You also were with Jesus the Nazarene." But he denied it, saying, "I neither know nor understand what you are talking about." And he went out onto the porch. The servant-girl saw him, and began once more to say to the bystanders, "This is one of them!" But again he denied it. And after a little while the bystanders were again saying to Peter, "Surely you are one of them, for you are a Galilean too." But he began to curse and swear, "I do not know this man you are talking about!" Immediately a rooster crowed a second time. And Peter remembered how Jesus had made the remark to him, "Before a rooster crows twice, you will deny Me three times." And he began to weep. (Mark 14: 53-54, 66-72)

So the Roman cohort and the commander and the officers of the Jews, arrested Jesus and bound Him, and led Him to Annas first; for he was father-in-law of Caiaphas, who was high priest that year. . . .

Simon Peter was following Jesus, and so was another disciple. Now that disciple was known to the high priest, and entered with Jesus into the court of the high priest, but Peter was standing at the door outside. So the other disciple, who was known by the high priest, went out and spoke to the doorkeeper, and brought Peter in. Then the slave-girl who kept the door said to Peter, "You are not also one of this man's disciples, are you?" He said, "I am not." Now the slaves and the officers were standing there, having made a charcoal fire, for it was cold and they were warming themselves;

and Peter was also with them, standing and warming himself. . . . So they said to him, "You are not also one of His disciples, are you?" He denied it, and said, "I am not."

One of the slaves of the high priest, being a relative of the one whose ear Peter cut off, said, "Did I not see you in the garden with Him?" Peter then denied it again, and immediately a rooster crowed. (John 18:12-18, 25-27)

IT IS IMPORTANT TO UNDERSTAND JOHN MARK WAS MORE THAN JUST an assistant to the Apostle Peter and the author of the first Gospel. He was also a pastor seeking to guide and comfort a Christian congregation in Rome that was being torn apart by Nero's persecution and sadistic cruelty. Christians were being arrested daily, tried for their faith, burned at the stake, fed to wild animals, beheaded, crucified, and hideously tortured. By the time he wrote his Gospel, even the Apostle Peter, and probably the Apostle Paul, had been martyred at the hands of Nero. Those were ghastly times.

Under the strain of those conditions, many Christians were cracking under the pressure. What would you do if soldiers broke into your home tonight and demanded: "Are you a Christian? If you are, we are going to torture your children in front of you until you disavow your faith." How would you respond?

When I was a child growing up in the Philippine Islands, I heard an old American missionary who had served in China tell a story that has haunted me for years. Shortly after World War II, this missionary returned to China to help the Chinese recover from the ravages of battle. No sooner had she arrived than the communist armies of Mao Tse-tung began to solidify their forces and conquer the land. The communists had a virulent hatred for all religion and sought to ruthlessly suppress every form of public worship.

For many months this missionary worked with a small Christian congregation in a rural village. When the communist forces approached the village, she was evacuated to a larger city. On the Sunday after her departure, when her friends met in the village to worship, communist troops appeared and surrounded the church. An officer marched in, took the Bible off the crude wooden altar, and threw it on the floor. He then told each person in the shocked congregation to walk by the Bible, step on it, and denounce their faith in Jesus Christ—or else pay a great price.

One by one the Chinese villagers walked by the Bible. If they placed their foot on the Bible, they were ushered outside the door of the church. If they refused to disclaim their faith, they were seated again in the church pews. When the last person had made their fateful decision, the communist officer marched brusquely out of the church, closing and padlocking the door behind him.

The communist troops surrounding the church set up machine guns directed at every entranceway. Then the church was doused with gasoline and set afire. All the Christians within the church were burned to death, a public example of what would happen to people with religious convictions. My missionary friend struggled for the rest of her life with survivor guilt. And she always wondered what she would have done if she had been in the congregation that day.

So it was in Rome. When arrested, if you disavowed your faith in Christ and bowed to worship the Roman emperor and his pantheon of gods, you and your family would be set free. If you did not recant your faith in Christ, you would meet a horrible death. Many Roman Christians lived with the guilt of publicly renouncing their faith, of becoming apostate. It was for these Christians that John Mark most wanted to tell the story of Peter's own denial of his relationship with Jesus. What was it that John Mark wanted to say?

All Christians Deny Christ

Perhaps while staring into a fire on a winter night, John Mark reflected on the great Apostle Peter's life. Within recent days Peter had paid the ultimate price for his faith. If Christian tradition is correct, Peter was publicly crucified by Nero, meeting the same fate as the Lord he had served for so many years. Peter had always been a man of great courage. And the Roman Christians loved and venerated this old and weathered "Prince of the Apostles."

Yet John Mark knew that this same man also had once crumbled under pressure and denied his relationship with Jesus. Peter had later talked openly of the incident. And though it was a painful subject, Peter obviously did not seek to keep it a secret. He couldn't, for it was public knowledge. Let's return to that fateful moment.

The cold of winter would have still lingered in the air of Jerusalem at Passover. Cloaked by darkness somewhere on the Mount of Olives, Peter and the other disciples were desperately hiding. Panting like flushed deer from their narrow escape, they felt their hearts pounding and watched their chilled breath float up toward a veiled harvest moon. Each of these shaken men stared intently as a line of flickering torches slowly snaked its way back across the Kidron Valley toward the high walls of Jerusalem. Jesus was now a prisoner of the Jewish Sanhedrin, a helpless puppet squeezed in the iron fist of Rome.

Slowly courage flowed back into Peter's heart. Peter and an unnamed disciple stood and began to follow the arresting party. Drawing close, they shadowed this hushed posse through the gates of Jerusalem and all the way to the high priest's residence in the Hasmonean palace, on the west hill, facing the Temple.[1] Standing in the street and staring at a closed and guarded gate, Peter's options ran out. But not so for the unnamed disciple. Whoever he was—John, Lazarus, Nicodemus, Joseph of Arimathea, to name a few candidates—this anonymous disciple was a friend of the high priest, Caiaphas, and had access to his palace.

As the guard at the gate granted Peter entrance into the courtyard, Peter knew that his actions were madness. He was thrusting his head into a hangman's noose. Yet he was determined to be with Jesus in this crisis.

Nervously warming himself by a charcoal fire, Peter was surrounded by the rowdy arrest party. Drawing his hooded cloak tightly around him, he hoped he would not be recognized. Peter desperately wanted to be left alone, to be silent and not be betrayed by his harsh Galilean accent.

Peter did not get his wish. Twice he was asked if he was a follower of Jesus', and he brusquely denied the accusation. Finally he was confronted by a woman who was related to the servant whose ear he had severed a few hours before. Seized by panic, he began to curse and insist, "I do not know this man you are talking about." Amidst the echo of his angry voice in the stone courtyard, the crow of a rooster was heard. John Mark concludes the scene with these poignant words: "And Peter remembered how Jesus had made the remark to him, 'Before a rooster crows twice, you will deny Me three times.' And he began to weep."

Many Roman Christians, decades after the crucifixion, wept the same bitter tears of remorse on the morning after they recanted their faith to save the lives of their family. In writing his Gospel, John Mark earnestly wanted them to see that even the greatest of Christians fail their Lord and, by their words and actions, scream out, "I don't know the man!"

Some years ago a college student called and made an appointment to talk with me. I had known him for many years, watched him grow up, baptized him, and knew that he was a fine Christian young man. But when he entered my office, I could tell that he was troubled and depressed.

After some small talk, there was an awkward silence. Then he blurted out: "Dr. Walker, I guess I've come here to make a confession. I've really screwed up." Then he launched into his story.

My young friend was a freshman at a large university and was pledging a fraternity. It seems that one night at a pledge party, he did something that he had never done before. He got very drunk. And when he did, his personality changed. A docile, polite young fellow became a roaring, raging, obnoxious fool. Picking a fight with a football player twice his size, he incited a free-for-all in a bar that resulted in his arrest. He was thrown into a jail cell to sober up and face the legal repercussions of his actions.

He was clear-headed and frightened by the time he was led to his jail cell, where the warden told him to take off his clothes and put on a bright orange prison uniform. Embarrassed, he slid off his shirt. The naked lightbulb of the prison cell glinted on the silver cross necklace he had worn since his baptism at the age of twelve. Quickly glancing up, he caught the warden staring at the silver cross too. Suddenly he "heard the rooster crow." He knew that he had betrayed far more than himself. He knew that when he chose to get drunk, strike another man in the face, and cause a riot, he had shouted to the world: "I do not know Jesus! I do not know that man!"

The bottom line is that as mature Christians, we come to realize that we all betray Jesus many times in our life. We all engage in activity in which our actions say, "I don't know him!"

Yesterday I read that the leading cause of death in our world is polluted and contaminated water. Do you realize how easy it would be for millions of Christians to significantly reduce this problem in a short period of time? We have the financial and technological resources to do so. And yet by our lack of action, we signify that we don't care. Unlike Jesus, we don't have concern for people who must drink the only water available to them and die of diseases that could easily be prevented. And when we don't care, when we are not galvanized into action by the need of our brothers and sisters, we shout to the world: "I don't know Jesus! I don't know the man!" We, his disciples, betray him.

It is true that the greatest saints are the ones who are most aware of their sinfulness, who often remember the moments when they denied that they ever knew Jesus. Betrayal is a part of the Christian pilgrimage. It happens to every one of us.

Failure Can Be the Seed of Success

As John Mark looked back over the course of Peter's long life, he realized that the rooster's crow was not only a note of condemnation but also a note of positive challenge. For while it is true that all Christians betray Christ, not all Christians react in the same way to their betrayal and resulting remorse.

It has often been noted that both Judas and Peter betrayed Jesus on the same night. Of course, this is not a just comparison, for their actions and intent were quite different. Yet both disciples were overcome by guilt and anguish for grievous mistakes they had made. Judas succumbed to shame and despair by committing suicide. Peter somehow managed to hang on and face one more day. How those two men chose to face their folly made all the difference as to whether personal failure led to defeat or triumph.

John Mark deeply desired to communicate to his fellow Christians that you cannot do something so bad or reprehensible that God cannot use the event to make you a better person. No shame is so dark, no action so cowardly, no vice so perverted that it can limit God's power to transform you. What will make all the difference is how you choose to react to failure and crisis.

For the rest of his life—indeed, until the present day—Peter's name is permanently connected to the words betrayal, denial, and desertion. Yet it is only against the contrast of this dark and shameful background that Peter's greatness can also be seen. By choosing to live through the shame and ignominy of a moment that history could not erase, Peter was able later to discover the meaning of the cross, the power of the resurrection, and the forgiving grace of God. Had Peter simply given up on himself and on God, his failure would have resulted not in life but in death.

As I reflect on my life, the Christians who have most influenced and encouraged me have not been the pious and overtly virtuous who seem never to have cursed or stumbled. I don't know how to relate to people like that, because I know they are not much like me. The men and women I most admire are Christians who have overcome great obstacles, been forgiven for flagrant sins, are open about their struggles and temptations, and do not make secret their complex humanity. Simon Peter was such a man. Because people could look at Peter in his later years and know that his betrayal did not destroy him, they gained courage to believe that their own betrayals of Christ need not crush them either. This was a message that the Christians in Rome desperately needed to hear. And it is good news for us to hear today as well.

Reflections
Psalms 32:5, 103:8-14; Luke 22:31-32; Romans 3:23; Hebrews 4:15-16

But now I had been beaten into the semblance of some kind of humility by misery and confusion and perplexity and secret, interior fear, and my ploughed soul was better ground for the reception of good seed.
   —*Thomas Merton*[2]

Every story of conversion is the story of a blessed defeat.
   —*C. S. Lewis*[3]

The wisest person is not the one who has the fewest failures, but the one who turns failures to best account.
   —*Richard R. Grant*[4]

How many failures have there been for one success, how many days of misery for one hour's joy, how many sins for a solitary saint?
   —*Pierre Teilhard de Chardin*[5]

To betray you must first belong.
    —*Harold Philby*[6]

Forgiveness is never a case of saying, "It's all right, it doesn't matter. . . ." There is nothing which brings a man to his senses with such arresting violence as to see the effect of his sin on someone who loves him in this world, or on God who loves him forever, and to say to himself: "It cost that to forgive my sin." Where there is forgiveness, someone must be crucified on a cross.
    —*William Barclay*[7]

I think that look of Christ might seem to say,
"Thou Peter! art thou, then, a common stone
Which I at last must break my heart upon,
For all God's charge to His high angels may
Guard my foot better? Did I yesterday
Wash *thy* feet, my beloved, that they should run
Quick to deny me 'neath the morning sun?
And do thy kisses, like the rest, betray?
The cock crows coldly, Go, and manifest
A late contrition, but no bootless fear;
For, when thy final need is dreariest,
Thou shalt not be denied, as I am here:
My voice to God and angels shall attest,
'Because *I know* this man, let him be clear.'"
    —*Elizabeth Barrett Browning*[8]

Dear Lord,

I have denied you before others many times. My betrayal has not always been the result of a flippant action or an impulsive decision. I confess that sometimes my denials have been deliberate, calculated, and habitual. Like Peter, I am a man of both strengths and weakness.

Yet I gain comfort in knowing that you understand me better than I understand myself. You know my frame and are mindful that I am dust. And you are aware, O Lord, that I long to be faithful to you.

God, forgive me when I have failed you and hurt others. May the cock-crow of my conscience stir me to greater resolve and lift me from despair. You are my Father, and I shall not fear the darkness. Amen.

Questions among Friends

1. Discuss some ways, by their actions or attitudes, that Christians frequently deny that they know Jesus.

2. Can you describe a moment when you "heard the rooster crow," and you knew that you had betrayed Christ?

3. Do you sometimes feel that God has not forgiven you for a time when you betrayed him? How can you better accept God's love and forgiveness?

4. What have you learned from this episode in Simon Peter's life?

Chapter Thirteen

GLIMPSING A NEW DIMENSION

Peter saw Jesus alive here (apparently)

❖

Now on the first day of the week Mary Magdalene came early to the tomb, while it was still dark, and saw the stone already taken away from the tomb. So she ran and came to Simon Peter and to the other disciple whom Jesus loved, and said to them, "They have taken away the Lord out of the tomb, and we do not know where they have laid Him." So Peter and the other disciple went forth, and they were going to the tomb. The two were running together; and the other disciple ran ahead faster than Peter and came to the tomb first; and stooping and looking in, he saw the linen wrappings lying there; but he did not go in. And so Simon Peter also came, following him, and entered the tomb; and he saw the linen wrappings lying there, and the face-cloth which had been on His head, not lying with the linen wrappings, but rolled up in a place by itself. So the other disciple who had first come to the tomb then also entered, and he saw and believed. For as yet they did not understand the Scripture, that He must rise again from the dead. So the disciples went away again to their own homes. (John 20:1-10)

For I delivered to you as of first importance what I also received, that Christ died for our sins according to the Scriptures, and that He was buried, and that He was raised on the third day according to the Scriptures, and that He appeared to Cephas, then to the twelve. After that He appeared to more than five hundred brethren at one time, most of whom remain until now, but some have fallen asleep; then He appeared to James, then to all the apostles; and last of all, as to one untimely born, He appeared to me also. (1 Corinthians 15:3-8)

Peter

WITH A ROOSTER'S CROW STILL SHRILL IN THE PREDAWN DARKNESS, the stage lights of John Mark's Gospel slowly fade on the silhouette of Peter. We, the audience, are left in shadow, wondering how Peter escaped from the high priest's palace, where he fled for safety, and how he endured the awful day of Jesus' crucifixion. The New Testament sheds no light on this mystery.

When the stage lights rise again on Peter's life, it is no longer John Mark's voice that is heard. Rather, it is the writer of the Gospel of John who now narrates the story. Consider for a moment how this scene might be depicted in a movie.

The moment is less than two days after Jesus' death, very early on a Sunday morning. The Sabbath has passed, and Peter escapes depression through fitful sleep. Suddenly his fragile truce with pain is shattered by the frightened voice of a woman, a voice that is familiar to him. Jolting awake, Peter realizes that the hysterical words belong to Mary Magdalene. She is screaming about a body being stolen. Jesus is not in the tomb, she is sobbing. Someone—the Sanhedrin, the Romans, grave robbers?—seems to have carried off the broken, shrouded corpse.

Still stiff from sleep, Peter and another disciple—referred to as *the beloved* disciple—hurry out to examine the tomb. Perhaps if the sun does not soon rise, they will not be seen, Peter hopes. But mostly he is immune to fear, numbed by tragedy.

Clambering up a steep path on a hillside pocked with tombs, Peter finds the scene as Mary described it. His fellow disciple has run ahead and is now peering in the entrance of the opened tomb, too spooked to enter. Peter impetuously brushes by him and waits for his eyes to adjust to the dimness of the cavern. He is relieved there is no stench, just the smell of burial spices softly wafting from the darkness.

Suddenly the hair on the back of Peter's neck prickles and stands on end. He realizes what his eyes are glimpsing through the dimness. It is the grave clothes. Long, broad strips of linen had draped the body of Jesus from head to foot. But though the body is clearly not present, the linen wrappings have not been stripped from the body and left strewn across the floor. Nor have they been neatly removed and folded. Rather, the wrappings have collapsed in place on the tomb shelf—collapsed as if the body had vaporized. Collapsed without being unwound. Only the face cloth has been rolled up and is lying to the side by itself. Peter and the beloved disciple look aghast at a scene they cannot fathom. As the writer of John simply concludes, the beloved disciple suddenly intuited the significance of the burial wrappings and "believed."

Resuscitation or Resurrection?

I will never forget a lecture I heard during my first year in seminary. It radically changed my life and thought. My professor was the acclaimed English New Testament scholar Dr. George Beasley-Murray, and he was teaching a course on the Gospel of John. On this day we were studying the resurrection of Jesus. I became riveted as Dr. Beasley-Murray discussed the nuances of the Greek words that described the burial wrappings of Jesus. He emphatically stated that it was the appearance of the grave clothes that caused the early disciples to first sense that something of momentous and incredible significance had happened. The condition of the linen wrappings was the disciples' first compelling clue that Jesus' body had not been stolen.

Another New Testament scholar, Dr. William Barclay, states the same position succinctly: "The grave-clothes were not disheveled and disarranged. They were lying there *still in their folds*—this is what the Greek means—the clothes for the body where the body had been; the napkin where the head had lain. The whole point of the description is that the grave-clothes did not look as if they had been put off or taken off; they were lying there in their regular folds as if the body of Jesus had simply evaporated out of them."[1]

When Dr. Beasley-Murray first led me to see this truth, my jaw dropped in amazement. For the first time, I realized the fundamental distinction between the *resuscitation* of a corpse and the *resurrection* of the dead. Until this distinction is made, one cannot understand Christianity. What is the difference?

Lazarus is the biblical example of a man who was resuscitated but not resurrected. When Jesus invoked the power of God to resuscitate Lazarus, four days of physical and biological decomposition was reversed. Lazarus's body was restored, just as it had been before he died. And when Lazarus walked forth from his tomb, he was easily recognized, because nothing about him had changed. Most significantly, Lazarus continued to age and grow older. One day he died again, only to be interred once more in a tomb.

Jesus' *resurrection*—and this is a technical term—was altogether different. Jesus' dead and decaying body was not resuscitated. It was totally transformed in a way that we cannot comprehend, for we have no mode of comparison. As the grave clothes collapsed, his body was transmuted into something it was not before. No longer was his body bound by time and space. He could appear and disappear, walk through a closed door and yet share in a meal with his disciples and eat solid food. At times those who saw him clearly recognized him, and at other times, he appeared to be a stranger. Above all, Jesus did not live to die again. Using words we cannot understand, he simply returned to his Father. He entered a realm we call "eternal life."

In future years the Apostle Paul wrestled with how to describe the resurrected Jesus. Paul used the terms "the body of His glory" or a "spiritual body" to depict what he could not explain.[2] Echoing Paul's terms, the esteemed biblical scholar F. F. Bruce concludes, "The body of flesh and blood, which was laid in the tomb, was evidently transmuted without remainder into His body of glory, in which he appeared to Peter, James and the others, and last of all to Paul himself."[3] What did this "body of glory" come to signify to Peter and other first-generation Christians?

The Fourth Dimension

Many Christians are surprised to discover that the earliest written report of the post-resurrection appearances of Jesus is not found in one of the four Gospels. Rather, it was written in A.D. 55 by the Apostle Paul, in a letter to the Christian Church in Corinth, ten years before the writing of the Gospel of Mark. Paul chronicles the post-resurrection appearances in this order: "He appeared to Cephas [Peter], then to the twelve. After that He appeared to more than five hundred brethren at one time, most of whom remain until now, but some have fallen asleep; then he appeared to James, then to all the apostles; and last of all, as to one untimely born, He appeared to me also" (1 Cor. 15:5-8).

It is strange that the Gospels do not describe an appearance of the resurrected Lord to Peter or to James, the brother of Jesus. But Paul is clear that at some point soon after the resurrection, Peter was the first to witness Jesus in his "glorified" form. When he did, Peter was confronted with a glimpse into a dimension of reality that he had never imagined. He was given insight into what we normally cannot see. Peter, in effect, briefly entered into a fourth dimension. What do I mean by "a fourth dimension"?

Let's reflect for a moment on the nature of the human eye. The human eye and the brain cooperate to form visual pictures of everything we see. By its physical construction, the human eye envisions all objects in three dimensions—height, depth, and width. Our eyes are limited to seeing reality only in those three dimensions.

Yet we must ask, "What if other dimensions exist, in addition to height, depth, and width—dimensions our human eyes and other sensory organs cannot discern? What if there are dimensions, like radio waves, that constantly but invisibly surround us but that cannot be comprehended unless we have a receiver that is not found in the human body? What if there are elements of reality all about us that cannot be perceived through our five senses? Does this mean that these other-dimensional realities do not exist? Not at all. It only means that we cannot perceive them.

When Jesus was resurrected by the power of God, he was transmuted into a dimension of reality that we cannot now know. And when we die, we are literally born into a deeper dimension of life that we cannot now perceive, a dimension we simply call *heaven.* The resurrection of Jesus was for Peter a glimpse into the fourth dimension, a gaze into ultimate reality.

I believe that the Apostle Paul shared these same thoughts. Living in what we call a prescientific age, Paul could not couch his thoughts in terms of our five senses or multidimensional perception. However, in 1 Corinthians 15:20, he states, "But now Christ has been raised from the dead, the first fruits of those who are asleep." In Colossians 1:15 and 18, he continues the metaphor, " [Jesus] is the image of the invisible God, the firstborn of all creation, . . . the firstborn from the dead." For Paul, the word *first* is central. He sees Jesus as the first person to introduce us to the fourth dimension through his resurrection. He sees Jesus as the one who by his resurrection gives us insight into what lies beyond the grave. Jesus is "the first fruits of those who are asleep."

A Vision of Hope

It was through his insight into the fourth dimension that a despondent and defeated Simon Peter was able to gain hope for the future. It was only through the startling and unexpected event of the resurrection that Peter and the disciples could again see any reason to believe that life is good and that the future bodes well for humanity. And, above all, that this future—this Good News!—cannot be thwarted by tragic events in human history. Years later Peter could look at the anguish of the Neronian persecution and know that even if all failed, if every Christian in Rome was killed, the future is still secure for those who follow Jesus.

Shortly before he died, the Apostle Peter dictated a brief letter to Christians in Rome. In his greeting he wrote, "Blessed be the God and Father of our Lord Jesus Christ, who according to His great mercy has caused us to be born again to a living hope through the resurrection of Jesus Christ from the dead, to obtain an inheritance which is imperishable and undefiled and will not fade away, reserved in heaven for you" (1 Peter 1:3-4). Peter was saying that it was through his experience of the resurrection of Jesus Christ that he had gained a "living hope," which was indestructible. No event on Earth could take it away. The fourth dimension could not be destroyed by Nero, by crucifixion, or by any other force.

One day when I was discouraged, I read *Out of Solitude,* by the late Father Henri Nouwen, a Catholic priest whose writings have often inspired me. Nouwen frequently wrestled with depression and disillusionment. But in this little book, Father Nouwen reminded me that it is our hope and expectations for the future that make all the difference in how we deal with inevitable moments of despair in the present. Nouwen writes:

The paradox of expectation indeed is that those who believe in tomorrow can better live today, that those who expect joy to come out of sadness can discover the beginnings of a new life in the center of the old, that those who look forward to the returning Lord can discover him already in their midst.

You know how a letter can change your day. When you watch people in front of a wall of mailboxes, you can see how a small piece of paper can change the expression on a face, can make a curved back straight, and a sullen mouth whistle again. . . . A life lived in expectation is like a life in which we have received a letter.[4]

The resurrection of Jesus Christ is a letter from God to all of his children. And the letter emphatically states that life is good and that death is but a false facade. It is a living letter that reveals that there is far more than we can presently know about our universe and that life is composed of limitless dimensions. It is wonderful news from our Father who promises that our future will always be very, very good.

Reflections
John 11:25-26, Romans 8:11, 1 Corinthians 15:51-52, 57

. . . . There have been times
when, after long on my knees
in a cold chancel, a stone has rolled
from my mind, and I have looked
in and seen the old questions lie
folded and in a place
by themselves, like the piled
graveclothes of a love's risen body.
—*R. S. Thomas*[5]

For the Christian, death does not extinguish the light. It puts out the lamp because the dawn has come.
—*Anonymous*

We must accept finite disappointment, but we must never lose infinite hope.
—*Martin Luther King Jr.*[6]

If I find in myself a desire which no experience in this world can satisfy, the most probable explanation is that I was made for another world.
—*C. S. Lewis*[7]

So sometimes comes to soul and sense
The feeling which is evidence
That very near about us lies
The realm of spiritual mysteries.
The sphere of the supernal powers
Impinges on this world of ours.
—*John Greenleaf Whittier*[8]

Dear Lord,

Sometimes I am like Simon Peter before dawn on Easter morning: hiding, terrified, sleeping away depression and void of hope. My pain is too real to believe that life can be good.

Wake me up, O Lord! Wake me up to the resurrection of my own faith. By your power transform me into someone I have never been before. Give me eyes to see beyond my limited world and to glimpse the goodness and glory of God.

Lord, awake me to discover my own grave clothes collapsed and empty. May I walk from my self-hewn tomb alive as never before. Amen.

Questions among Friends

1. Can you remember when you first understood that Jesus did not experience a resuscitation but rather a resurrection? How has this discovery affected you?

2. Have you ever felt that you have caught a glimpse of or gained insight into "the fourth dimension"?

3. Describe an occasion—perhaps one of many occasions—when you realized that Jesus is alive and that the faith of Christianity is true.

4. Discuss Henri Nouwen's statement, *"The paradox of expectation indeed is that those who believe in tomorrow can better live today, that those who expect joy to come out of sadness can discover the beginnings of a new life in the center of the old."* Can you give an example of someone you know who exemplifies such hope and positive expectation?

Chapter Fourteen

"FEED MY SHEEP"

After these things Jesus manifested himself again to the disciples at the Sea of Tiberias, and he manifested Himself in this way. . . .

But when the day was now breaking, Jesus stood on the beach; yet the disciples did not know that it was Jesus. . . .

Jesus said to them, "Bring some of the fish which you have now caught." Simon Peter went up and drew the net to land, full of large fish, a hundred and fifty-three; and although there were so many, the net was not torn. Jesus said to them, "Come and have breakfast." None of the disciples ventured to question Him, "Who are You?" knowing that it was the Lord. Jesus came and took the bread and gave it to them, and the fish likewise. This is now the third time that Jesus was manifested to the disciples, after He was raised from the dead.

So when they had finished breakfast, Jesus said to Simon Peter, "Simon, son of John, do you love Me more than these?" Peter said to Him, "Yes, Lord; You know that I love You." He said to him, "Tend My lambs." He said to him again a second time, "Simon, son of John, do you love Me?" He said, "Yes Lord; You know that I love You." He said to him, "Shepherd My sheep." He said to him the third time, "Simon, son of John, do you love Me?" Peter was grieved because He said to him the third time, "Do you love me?" And he said to Him, "Lord, You know all things; You know that I love You." Jesus said to him, "Tend My sheep. Truly, truly, I say to you, when you were younger, you used to gird yourself and walk wherever you wished; but when you grow old, you will stretch out your hands and someone else will gird you, and bring you where you do not wish to go." Now this He said, signifying by what kind of death he would glorify God. And when He had spoken this, He said to him, "Follow Me!" (John 21:1, 4, 10-19)

PRIOR TO THIS EARLY MORNING BREAKFAST ON THE SHORE OF THE Sea of Galilee, Peter had already met the resurrected Jesus. As noted earlier, Paul tells us in 1 Corinthians 15:5 that Peter was one of the first to whom Jesus appeared. In addition, the Gospel of John relates that Jesus was manifested to all the disciples twice before the present encounter on the seashore. Thus, although Peter may have been frightened when confronted by the specter of Jesus preparing breakfast over an open fire, he would not have been totally surprised or unbelieving.

Still, to stand in the presence of the risen Jesus must have been an unnerving and eerie experience. For Peter it was awkward and embarrassing as well. After all, Jesus was a dear friend whom Peter had blatantly betrayed. And this breached relationship had not been restored. Peter was in desperate need of forgiveness. To be separated by broken trust from a person whom you love is a pain that is not easily borne.

Our Need of Forgiveness

Every one of us—saint or criminal—harbors within us a spiritual and existential need for forgiveness; to feel that despite having made major mistakes, we are worthy of God's love and acceptance. To put it another way, after years of living, we all desire to see our face in a mirror and be able to smile rather than wince.

For people who have never done anything radically wrong, this is sometimes a difficult truth to understand. I reflect on my own life and remember when I was eight years old and was considering being baptized as a Christian. It seemed that for the last few months, the dominant theme that I had heard from my pastor and my Sunday school teachers was that all people—my young self included—were sinners and in need of forgiveness. I must admit that as a child, I was not aware of, or plagued by, a sense of sinfulness. Nor should I have been. But if these adults said I was a sinner and that I needed to be forgiven, I was willing to take their word for it. But I had little recognition of truth in my blind surrender to their teaching.

In my fifties, my perspective is quite different. A lot of water has gone under the bridge since childhood. I have had adequate time to make my fair share of mistakes. I have lost the sense of innocence. I have learned that I often separate myself relationally from God by my actions and attitudes. And I need a bridge to connect me to God.

I recently read a moving story written by Glenn Tinder, a professor of political science, who describes his own growing awareness of a need for forgiveness from, and reconciliation with, God. Glenn was reared in a devout home. His mother was of Quaker descent, and in her adult years, she was deeply influenced by the teachings of Christian Science. From birth Glenn was surrounded by religious piety and was a good and conscientious young man. Still, when he graduated from high school, Glenn was not a Christian.

As Glenn entered early adulthood, he faced a world consumed by the destruction of World War II. Enlisting in the United States Navy, Glenn was assigned to the crew of a large landing ship in the Pacific, primarily in the Philippine Islands. In 1945 Glenn's ship sailed into Manila Harbor to discover a city ravaged by war. Though actual combat had moved north of Manila, Japanese stragglers and snipers remained, and there was a constant sense of lurking danger.

In Manila Harbor were dozens of Japanese cargo ships, which had been sunk by American planes. Though their hulls rested on the bottom of the harbor, their superstructures still remained above the waterline, creating eerie silhouettes at sunset. Many of the American sailors, bored by backwater duty, itched to explore these rusting hulks to find souvenirs and even treasure. It was rumoured, however, that Japanese stragglers were holed up in these ships and would be dangerous if found.

One day Glenn and some of his buddies could resist temptation no longer. They set off on a small boat to explore a large sunken freighter. It was a moment that would change Glenn's life:

> We had gone through two or three ships and were tying up our boat at the side of another. Suddenly there was shattering gunfire right at my side. One of our sailors had seen a Japanese soldier on the ship, only 20 or 30 feet away. . . .
>
> Trembling with fear we went aboard. We thought the Japanese soldier had been hit and probably killed, but we weren't sure, he might still be alive, and he might have companions. I crept up to a porthole and looked into a cabin where we thought the soldier might be in the semidarkness. I seemed to see a figure on the deck, perhaps reclining against a bulkhead. Shielding myself as fully as possible, I reached through the porthole and fired several times. We found the soldier, indeed dead, in the cabin into which I had fired. He was unarmed.

The thought that he had possibly shot a starving, unarmed man did not immediately worry Glenn. Those were days of war. However, it was not long before a sense of guilt began to hound him. Though he learned to cope with his inner anguish and chagrin, the feelings of remorse—the gnawing awareness that he had done something wrong—never left him. "I realized that I had committed an offense against something holy and, as far as I knew, remorseless and unforgiving."[1]

Returning from the war, Glenn entered college and immersed himself in scholarship. Though not an atheist, he did not claim to be a Christian. Voraciously he read Plato, Søren Kierkegaard, Karl Jaspers, Gabriel Marcel, Nicolas Berdyaev, Fyodor Dostoevsky, Martin Buber, Karl Barth, and many other great thinkers. Each of these men gave him insight into human nature and the existential dilemmas of life. Glenn Tinder came to know that the seminal cause of human pain is a profound awareness that our sins have separated us relationally and emotionally from the source of our being, from our Creator God.

During the next twenty years, Glenn also recognized that at the center of the Christian message are the themes of forgiveness and reconciliation. Christianity is the good news that no amount of sin or mistakes can hinder a person from being reconciled with God. Faced with this good news—and deeply wanting forgiveness—Glenn recognized that, like a moth, he had slowly been drawn to this flickering Christian candle of truth and hope. One day he simply awoke to realize that he was a Christian, that he had been reconciled with and forgiven by God. "Christian existence, one must also remember, is a drama of estrangement (for me, Christian Science) and reconciliation of sin (Manila Bay) and redemption. . . . But God does not forgive us just for grave misdeed, long repented of, such as those I committed in Manila Bay. He forgives us, I believe, minute by minute, in response to the continuing stream of minor and not-so-minor misdeeds that, for most us, mark the course of our fallen lives."[2]

Just as Peter stood on a shoreline centuries ago realizing how separated he was from Jesus, so do we. Now we are seasoned adults, and we know exactly what the Apostle Paul meant when he wrote, "All have sinned and fallen short of the glory of God" (Romans 3:23). To slowly come to this awareness that we are not all that we want to be—that we have "missed the mark"—is an inevitable and healthy part of maturing as a Christian disciple. And such knowledge is the key to spiritual freedom.

With Peter, we become free on the day we realize that we have a profound need to be forgiven. And, paradoxically, we become free when we discover that God's love and forgiveness are never ending.

Self-Forgiveness Actualized by Love

After breakfast Jesus approached Peter for a serious conversation. The future of Peter's life depended on the outcome of the next few moments. Holding Peter in his steady gaze, Jesus demanded in a formal way, "Simon, son of John, do you love Me more than these?"

Jesus' words stung Peter. They cut through all pretense. Instantly Peter heard the echo of his own proud voice only hours before he betrayed Jesus:

"Even though all may fall away, yet I will not. . . . Even if I have to die with You, I will not deny You!" (Mark 14:29-31).

Now Jesus was saying: "Peter, were you stronger than all the rest? Were you immune to sin? Was your strength adequate to make sin cower? No, it obviously was not. But that is not what is most important. I want to know only one thing. Do you love me?"

Cut down to size, Peter blurted, "Yes, Lord; You know that I love You." Jesus simply said, "Tend My lambs."

Hardly had Jesus' voice faded when Peter was jolted by a second question, identical to the first. Obviously Jesus was now going for the jugular. "Simon, son of John, do you love Me?" Peter, perhaps more emphatically, echoed his first reply, "Yes, Lord; You know that I love You." But this time Jesus altered his reply: "Shepherd My sheep."

Seizing Peter firmly with his eyes, Jesus drew closer, like a trial lawyer honing in on a verdict, with dramatic speech, deliberate cadence, and the power of pithy repetition: "Simon, son of John, do you love Me?" Stunned by the salvo of the third identical question, Peter no doubt heard the crow of the rooster as he remembered Jesus' prophecy that Peter would betray him three times. Jesus' threefold emphasis was lost on no one. Three betrayals and three questions; and each time the same response: "Tend My lambs. . . . Shepherd My sheep. . . . Tend My sheep."

Was Jesus simply being mean? Was he rubbing salt in a wound or kicking a helpless dog? No, to the contrary, Jesus loved Peter so much that he knew if he did not get Peter's full attention—did not nail down one eternal truth—Peter would never survive his own grief and pain. What was this truth? Precisely this: *Only our ability and desire to love others will release us from the bondage of our own guilt and remorse.*

The late Dr. Lewis Smedes, of Fuller Theological Seminary, had insight into the human soul and psyche that is rare and profound. In his book *Forgive and Forget*, Smedes correctly recognizes that the best way to be released from the guilt of our own sinfulness is to live a life of loving others. Such love toward others is not an act of penance for our sins, a love that is duty and obligation. Rather, such love is an act of freedom that comes through the joy of the discovery that you—the real you, warts and all—are loved and accepted by God. Listen to the wisdom of Lewis Smedes:

> Do you dare release the person you are today from the shadow of the wrong you did yesterday? . . . Where do you get the right—let alone the cheek—to forgive yourself when other people would want you to crawl in shame if they really knew? How dare you?
>
> The answer is that you get the right to forgive yourself only from the entitlements of love. And you dare forgive yourself only with the courage

of love. . . . How can you know for sure that you gambled with guilt and won unless you gamble your winnings on love? . . . Love is a signal that you have done it, that you have actually released the guilt that condemned you. You won't always know exactly when you have forgiven yourself. It is like reaching the top of a long hill on a highway—you may not be sure when you have reached level ground, but you can tell that you have passed the top when you step on the gas and the car spurts ahead. An act of love is like quick acceleration. A free act of love, to anyone at all, may signal to you that you do, after all, have the power that comes to anyone who is self-for-giving. . . . Yes, love gives you the right to forgive yourself. And it gives you the power as well.[3]

Jesus knew that Peter was a man of principle and integrity. Peter's great-est spiritual danger was that he might never forgive himself for his human weakness and destroy himself like Judas did. Jesus therefore "got in his face" and told him forcefully of the only way he could be healed of guilt. He pre-scribed for Peter a two-part formula. First, love God with all your heart ("Simon, son of John, do you love Me?"). And second, love your neighbor as yourself ("Tend My sheep."). If such love of others is done in freedom and joy, guilt will melt away.

THE WRITER OF THE GOSPEL OF JOHN KNEW THAT WITHIN CHRISTIAN communities scattered throughout the Mediterranean world were thousands of Christians who were struggling with accepting the forgiveness of a loving God. Some could not forgive themselves for recanting their faith in the midst of persecution. Some had slid into old sensuous habits fostered by pagan religions. The reasons were myriad, but the result was the same. When Christians do not freely and joyfully accept God's forgiveness, Satan uses their guilt to beat them to a spiritual pulp.

We are entitled by God's love—demonstrated on the cross of Jesus—to accept that we are forgiven again and again and again. God's forgiveness is as endless as his love. And his forgiveness can be our motivation to joyfully love others.

Reflections

Nehemiah 9:16-20, Psalm 86:5, Isaiah 55:6-8, Matthew 22:35-40, Romans 8:1-2, 1 John 1:9, 3:23

I think that if God forgives us we must forgive ourselves. Otherwise it is almost like setting up ourselves as a higher tribunal than Him.
   —*C. S. Lewis*[4]

Forgiveness is the answer to the child's dream of a miracle by which what is broken is made whole again, what is soiled is again made clean. The dream explains why we need to be forgiven, and why we must forgive. In the presence of God, nothing stands between Him and us—we *are* forgiven. But we *cannot* feel His presence if anything is allowed to stand between ourselves and others.
   —*Dag Hammarskjöld*[5]

During the past year a great joy has befallen me. Difficult though it is, I shall try to explain this in words.
   It is astonishing that sometimes we believe that we believe what, really, in our heart, we do not believe.
   For a long time I believed that I believed in the forgiveness of sins. But suddenly (on St. Mark's Day) this truth appeared in my mind in so clear a light that I perceived that never before (and that after many confessions and absolutions) had I believed it with my whole heart.
   So great is the difference between mere affirmation by the intellect and that faith, fixed in the very marrow and as it were palpable, which the Apostle wrote was *substance.*
   —*C. S. Lewis*[6]

We pardon as long as we love.
   —*L. A. Rochefoucauld*[7]

Dear Father,
   I am much like Simon Peter—impetuous, headstrong, charismatic, passionate, full of sound and fury. I have lived life fully, faced seismic storms, pressed the boundaries, kept the rules and broken them, had my good days and bad. Through it all I have tried to follow my Lord, Jesus. But there are days when I have wandered lost, and stumbled from your presence. I know what it is to sin, O Lord. And to repent, and to sin again. I grow weary of my excuses, the hollow sound of renewed resolve, the sighs of my own broken heart.
   And yet, I know, O Father, that you love me. You love me when I do not love myself. You love me because you are purest love. You embrace me because I am your child and you are my Father. Nothing more needs to be said.

Lord, save me from the ravages of self-despising guilt. Transform my remorse into love for others. May I be faithful to tend your sheep and discover the joy that only a shepherd can know. Amen.

Questions among Friends

1. Do you sometimes struggle with a pervading sense of guilt? How have you learned to cope with your guilt or find release from your guilt?

2. Share a time when the power of evil used guilt to tear you down and separate you from God. When was guilt a destructive influence in your life?

3. Discuss the two-part formula for diminishing guilt that Jesus gave to Peter:

    a. Love God with all your heart ("Simon, . . . do you love Me?").

    b. Love your neighbor as yourself ("Tend My sheep.").

4. After reading this chapter, have you become aware of a person whom you need to love, a sheep that you need to shepherd?

5. How has God's Spirit spoken to you as you read the pages of this chapter?

Chapter Fifteen

"WHAT I DO HAVE
I GIVE TO YOU"

Now Peter and John were going up to the temple at the ninth hour, the hour of prayer. And a man who had been lame from his mother's womb was being carried along, whom they used to set down every day at the gate of the temple which is called Beautiful, in order to beg alms of those who were entering the temple. When he saw Peter and John about to go into the temple, he began asking to receive alms. But Peter, along with John, fixed his gaze on him and said, "Look at us!" And he began to give them his attention, expecting to receive something from them. But Peter said, "I do not possess silver and gold, but what I do have I give to you: In the name of Jesus Christ the Nazarene—walk!" And seizing him by the right hand, he raised him up; and immediately his feet and his ankles were strengthened. With a leap, he stood upright and began to walk; and he entered the temple with them, walking and leaping and praising God. And all the people saw him walking and praising God; and they were taking note of him as being the one who used to sit at the Beautiful Gate of the temple to beg alms, and they were filled with wonder and amazement at what had happened to him. (Acts 3:1-10)

As we move beyond the earthly ministry of Jesus and his reunification with God the Father, we find Peter living and ministering in Jerusalem. No longer are the writers of the Gospels of Mark, Matthew, and John telling Peter's life story. Rather, they end their Gospels with the conclusion of Jesus' ministry. Only the writer of the Gospel of Luke continues to narrate the story of the first generation of Christians. Concluding the Gospel of Luke, he then writes a second volume, the Acts of the Apostles. It is to the Acts of the Apostles, and portions of Paul's collected epistles, that we now turn to cast a spotlight on Peter's mature adult years.

❧

IT IS CLEAR FROM THE GOSPEL RECORD THAT DURING JESUS' MINISTRY, Peter was one of the dominant personalities among the disciples. Indeed, Peter and the two sons of Zebedee, James and John, seemed to have formed an inner circle that was closest to Jesus, and took leadership roles among their fellow disciples. This trend continued after Jesus' death. As the Acts of the Apostles begins, Peter moves into the primary leadership role among the followers of Jesus in Jerusalem. The Apostle John often accompanies Peter, but plays a secondary and supportive role to Peter the Rock.

It is not clear how soon after Pentecost our present scene took place. However, early in Luke's account, Peter and John are involved in an incident of defining importance at one of the Temple gates. How they handle this situation will set the stage for the future of Christian ministry.

The scene begins on a weekday at three o'clock in the afternoon. Three times each day—at 9 A.M., noon, and 3 P.M.—devout Jews in Jerusalem would stop whatever they were doing and either go to the Temple or turn and face the Temple for a time of prayer. On this day Peter and John were rushing to the Temple for the three o'clock prayer when they were stopped at one of the Temple gates by a beggar asking for alms.

As a boy growing up in the Philippines, I remember that relating to beggars was part of my everyday life. Each day, impoverished families would bring blind and maimed children or grandparents with hideous diseases into the city and lay them on blankets near public places. I recall that when I accompanied my father to the post office, we would walk past dozens of beggars, each pitifully calling for help. At the end of the day, the family members of the beggars would come and take them home. It was a tragic but accepted part of Filipino culture.

So it was in Jerusalem. Peter and John were so used to seeing the hordes of beggars clustered at the Temple gates that it would have been natural for them to walk briskly by. But on this day a certain beggar snared their attention. The beggar was a man forty years of age who had been lame from birth.[1] Having succeeded in stopping Peter and John, he contritely bowed his head to beg for mercy and reached out his hand to receive money. Peter stopped and made a spontaneous decision. With perhaps a commanding voice, Peter demanded, "Look at us!" When the beggar raised his eyes, Peter "fixed his gaze on him" and said words that echo through Christian history: "I do not possess silver and gold, but what I do have I give to you: In the name of Jesus Christ the Nazarene—walk!"

For a moment the man sat with his arm still outstretched. Peter reached down, grasped his arm, and pulled him up. Suddenly "his feet and his ankles were strengthened." The man began to stumble, then walk, and even leap.

Like a grateful stray puppy, he eagerly followed Peter and John into the Temple, telling all who would listen what had happened. What can we learn today from this simple story about Christian discipleship and ministry?

Stopping: The First Step toward Healing

We can assume that as Peter's eyes first focused on the imploring face of the beggar, Peter intuitively felt a need to respond. He stopped and perhaps wondered for a split second what he should do. Then the experience of following Jesus for three years prodded him. Peter knew what he should do. He should respond just as Jesus would have responded. Jesus would have reached out and somehow helped this man.

As simple as it sounds, the decision to *stop* and help a person is at the heart of Christian discipleship. Every day God places someone in our path who is in need. When Peter glimpsed this crippled man, he knew that he was being thrown into the quandary of decision. He could either stop or go attend to his prayers in the Temple.

As I write these words, my home in Waco, Texas, is being buffeted by a severe winter ice storm. It is most unusual weather for our temperate region of the state. I was not prepared for this, and as the sky grew dark and the temperature plummeted this afternoon, I stopped on my way home to stock up on groceries. As I entered the supermarket, I saw a middle-aged man standing just inside the door. He was unkempt, dirty, and shabbily dressed. I realized that I had seen him many times, aimlessly walking the streets, obviously homeless and poor. I walked past him and went about my business.

Thirty minutes later, as I guided my full grocery cart toward the parking lot, I saw the man again, still huddled by the door, trying to stay out of the freezing rain. As I passed by him, he did not say a word. He didn't even look at me. He was lost in another hazy world.

As I walked to my car, sleet was blowing in my face. I hurriedly loaded the groceries, but as I did so, I could not stop thinking about the man. Suddenly I knew that on this cold night, I could not walk by him. Stepping back inside the warmth of the grocery store, I walked up to the man and, fumbling for words, heard my unsure voice ask, "Where you staying tonight?" Struggling through an alcoholic fog, he mumbled, "Salvation Army, down the street." For a moment it was quiet. Then I said, "Do you have money for supper?" He looked down at the floor and shook his head. He didn't have a penny to his name. I reached in my pocket, fumbled for a couple of bills, and handed them to him. But then I paused. I felt like something more should be said. Even though I am a pastor, words do not come easily. Finally, I awkwardly placed my hand on his shoulder and said the only thing that seemed natural, "God bless you, buddy." Suddenly he looked up through his stupor and reached way back to something in his past. His face broke into a toothless grin, and with deep feeling, he said, "God bless you too, my friend." I offered him a ride, but he didn't want one. He didn't want to move. We just said good-bye, and I walked away.

The first step in bringing somebody toward health is *stopping* long enough to see them. This is where Christian ministry begins. It can only begin when we pause long enough to see the need of the person that God has placed in our path.

Caring: The Second Step toward Healing

Reading the story about Peter and the lame beggar makes me wish that somehow I could have healed the man in the grocery store—healed him of alcoholism and mental illness and emphysema and a dozen other ills. But either I can't or I didn't do it. Yet, lest I be too hard on myself, I must remember that the first step to healing a person is stopping, and the second step is caring.

It is a fact that not all illnesses can be healed on this side of eternity. Disease and death are a part of life. Even Jesus did not attempt to eradicate all disease from the world. But he did stop and care for the men and women he met each day. And somehow his focused caring brought healing to their life.

The gifted priest Henri Nouwen once preached to a gathering of students at Yale University. Many of these young adults were "the brightest and best," who would become the next generation of doctors, ministers, research scientists, political leaders, and teachers. They would be the ones with the opportunity to heal the world of disease and strife and pain. Listen to what Nouwen said to them:

> When we honestly ask ourselves which persons in our lives mean the most to us, we often find that it is those who, instead of giving much advice, solutions, or cures, have chosen rather to share our pain and touch our wounds with a gentle and tender hand. The friend who can be silent with us in a moment of despair or confusion, who can stay with us in an hour of grief and bereavement, who can tolerate not-knowing, not-curing, not-healing and face with us the reality of our powerlessness, that is the friend who cares.

Then, after establishing the priority of caring, Nouwen brought his message to a climax with a subtle allusion to Peter and the lame beggar at the Temple gate:

Why is it that we keep that great gift of care so deeply hidden? Why is it that we keep giving dimes without daring to look into the face of the beggar? Why is it that we do not join the lonely eater in the dining hall but look for those we know so well? Why is it that we so seldom knock on a door or grab a phone, just to say hello, just to show that we have been thinking about each other? Why are smiles still hard to get and words of comfort so difficult to come by? Why is it so hard to express thanks to a teacher, admiration to a student, and appreciation to the men and women who cook, clean, and garden? Why do we keep bypassing each other always on the way to something or someone more important?[2]

The fact is that you can stop to help but simply not care. You can stop to do your Christian duty but not really empathize with the person. As a pastor I am often haunted by this truth. Frequently my assistant gives me a list of a dozen people I need to visit in the hospital, and I dash off to complete my checklist. I certainly do not want to get into trouble by being negligent of my flock. So I rush down the hospital corridors, sticking my head into doorways, smiling brightly, saying the expected prayers for healing, and above all communicating that I am a busy man in a big hurry. I have stopped at each hospital room. But have I cared?

Somehow when Peter looked at the lame beggar whose eyes were cast down and he said "Look at us!" the beggar instantly knew that this man had done more than stop. He also cared. The Christian disciple is one who both stops and cares. And these two actions set the stage for healing.

Inviting the Presence of God: The Third Step toward Healing

When the beggar looked up, he expected to receive money. He did not anticipate Peter's words: "I do not possess silver and gold, but what I do have I give to you: In the name of Jesus Christ the Nazarene—walk!" What was Peter doing? What was Peter saying?

In the ancient world, to formally invoke the name of a king or a god was to literally call forth the spiritual presence or personality of that distant king or god into the very space—the specific situation—being addressed. Peter, in calling forth the name of Jesus Christ the Nazarene, was asking for the presence of Jesus to be in their midst and to bring healing.[3]

Peter was clear about one thing: he knew that he did not have the power to heal the beggar. But Peter had also learned through following Jesus that asking for God's presence to be joined with human caring can bring healing into people's lives.

I remember a time when, as a young man, I was going through spiritual and emotional paralysis in my own life. I had graduated from college a year before, and was now struggling to find direction in my life. I knew I wanted to go to graduate school, but was fearful of making decisions. I was trying to choose between law school, seminary, and a career in theater and music. The more I tried to decide between these equally attractive options, the more confused I became. And with the confusion came a paralyzing sense of depression.

I needed a father to talk with, but my own father had been dead for nearly ten years. Finally, I called my godparents, Bryant and Peggy Hicks, and asked them if I could fly to their home in Louisville, Kentucky, and spend the weekend with them. They could tell that I was struggling, so they cancelled their plans and warmly invited me to come.

On the last night of my visit, Peggy had prepared a wonderful dinner, and we were sitting around the table deep in discussion. Finally, Bryant reached over and took my hand in his big paw—the first time a man had held my hand in a long time. Then Peggy took my other hand, and Bryant said: "Scott, I think we need to pray about these big decisions in your life and for your own emotional healing. As I pray I am going to ask God to be with us and to give us guidance." Then Bryant began to pray for me.

I do not want to overdramatize the moment, because tongues of fire did not dart around the room, and we did not begin to speak in the voices of Pentecost. But what I can tell you was that suddenly all the tears of a lifetime began to silently roll down my cheeks, and I felt the presence of God in the room and in the midst of our prayer. I did not suddenly receive great visions of what lay in store for my future nor did I instantly make a vocational decision. But I did become keenly aware of a sense of peace washing over me. I did not know what my future held, but I did feel that God was with me and that everything would be all right. On that night I began to be healed of an emotional and spiritual paralysis that had plagued me for months. My legs grew strong again. I felt that I could leap with joy.

Thirty years later I remain convinced that I would not have experienced this spiritual healing and direction if Bryant and Peggy Hicks had not stopped their busy lives to take time with me; if they had not cared deeply for me; and if they had not physically taken my hands, asked for God's presence in our lives, and prayed with me. I know this because I was once a beggar who was spiritually set free.

The Unique Contribution of Christianity

More than any other disciple of Jesus', Peter defined most clearly the unique contribution of Christianity to a hurting world when he said, "I do not possess silver or gold, but what I do have I give to you: In the name of Jesus Christ the Nazarene—walk!"

What Christianity has to give to the world is reunification with God through Jesus Christ. This does not mean that Christians should not use silver and gold to help relieve suffering. Far from it. Christians should use far more monetary means than we do to feed the hungry, heal the sick, support education, and lift up the oppressed. However, if we ever lose sight of the fact that all the things money can buy are empty if people are not connected to the presence and power of the Spirit of God, then Christians have wasted their efforts.

Millions of Christians could radically change our world in a short time if we would follow Peter's threefold approach to healing:

. . . *Stop* when people in need cross your path.
. . . *Care* deeply for the person you stop to help.
. . . *Invite* the presence of God to heal their lives.

make cards for all in class with it they on it

Reflections

Isaiah 35:4-6, Matthew 7:12, Luke 10:30-37

A few years ago I met an old professor at the University of Notre Dame. Looking back on his long life of teaching, he said with a funny twinkle in his eyes: "I have always been complaining that my work was constantly interrupted, until I slowly discovered that my interruptions were my work."
—*Henri J. M. Nouwen*[4]

Now the whole offer which Christianity makes is this: that we can, if we let God have His way, come to share in the life of Christ. . . . Christ is the Son of God. If we share in this kind of life we also shall be sons of God. We shall love the Father as he does and the Holy Ghost will arise in us. . . . Every Christian is to become a little Christ. The whole purpose of becoming a Christian is simply nothing else.
—*C. S. Lewis*[5]

There are, no doubt, passages in the New Testament which may seem at first sight to promise an invariable granting of our prayers. But that cannot be what they really mean. For in the very heart of the story we meet a glaring instance to the contrary. In Gethsemane the holiest of all petitioners prayed three times that a certain cup might pass from Him. It did not. After that the idea that prayer is recommended to us as a sort of infallible gimmick may be dismissed.
    —*C. S. Lewis*[6]

To feel sorry for the needy is not the mark of a Christian—to help them is.
    —*Frank A. Clark*[7]

Sick or well, blind or seeing, bond or free, we are here for a purpose, and however we are situated, we please God better with useful deeds than with many prayers of pious resignation.
    —*Helen Keller*[8]

He has not hands but our hands
To do His work today;
He has not feet but our feet,
To lead men in His way;
He has no voice but our voice
To tell men how He died;
He has no help but our help
To lead them to His side.
    —*Anonymous*

Dear Father,
    Help me today not to be so busy that I do no good. Help me to see your hurting child that you have sent my way. May I not fear to touch them and pray your blessing on their life. And, Lord, may I too be healed through helping others. Amen.

Questions among Friends

1. Share a time when you decided to stop and care for someone who was in need. Also, share a time when perhaps you should have stopped and did not. Why do you think that stopping to care is often so difficult? What makes you hesitate to do so?

2. Describe a moment when someone else cared for you, prayed for you, and helped bring the presence of God into your life.

3. How has helping others brought healing to your own life? Can you give an example?

4. Do you have a need in your life today that you can ask your friends to pray for?

Chapter Sixteen

DEADLY SINS

But a man named Ananias, with his wife Sapphira, sold a piece of property, and kept back some of the price for himself, with his wife's full knowledge, and bringing a portion of it, he laid it at the apostles' feet. But Peter said, "Ananias, why has Satan filled your heart to lie to the Holy Spirit and to keep back some of the price of the land? While it remained unsold, did it not remain your own? And after it was sold, was it not under your control? Why is it that you have conceived this deed in your heart? You have not lied to men but to God." And as he heard these words, Ananias fell down and breathed his last; and great fear came over all who heard of it. The young men got up and covered him up, and after carrying him out, they buried him.

Now there elapsed an interval of about three hours, and his wife came in, not knowing what had happened. And Peter responded to her, "Tell me whether you sold the land for such and such a price?" And she said, "Yes, that was the price." Then Peter said to her, "Why is it that you have agreed together to put the Spirit of the Lord to the test? Behold, the feet of those who have buried your husband are at the door, and they will carry you out as well."

And immediately she fell at his feet and breathed her last, and the young men came in and found her dead, and they carried her out and buried her beside her husband. And great fear came over the whole church, and over all who heard of these things. (Acts 5:1-11)

YOU HAVE JUST READ ONE OF THE MOST DIFFICULT, CONFUSING, AND troubling passages in the New Testament. Indeed, it is such a difficult passage that I initially chose not to include it in this study of Simon Peter. But the message in this story is so powerful—and so important to the theme of Christian discipleship—that it must be included.

Why the difficulty? First, let's understand the story. Ananias and Sapphira were a married couple who were part of the earliest Christian community in Jerusalem. Jewish Christians were increasingly being looked on as suspicious and strange by their fellow Jews, even though Christianity at this time was not regarded as a religious faith separate from Judaism. In fact, the term *Christians* had not yet been coined. This title was first used in reference to the followers of Jesus in Antioch about ten years later.[1] Rather, Peter and his fellow Jewish Christians simply saw themselves as orthodox Jews who also believed that the Messiah had come in the person of Jesus Christ. It would only be in future years that Christianity would separate from Judaism as a distinct though intimately related religious faith.

Yet, as our story unfolds, the conflict and division were beginning to build. Christians were being ostracized and discriminated against for their messianic views. Such discrimination led directly to financial oppression. Circumstances became so difficult that the followers of Jesus chose a form of communal living. Acts 2:44-45 states, "And all those who had believed were together and had all things in common; and they began selling their property and possessions and were sharing them with all, as anyone might have need."

It is in this context that Ananias and Sapphira step on the stage. Evidently Ananias had announced that he was selling a piece of personal property and would give all the proceeds to the Christian community. Such an action was laudable and appreciated. Once he sold the land, however, Ananias apparently cooked up a scheme. He sold the property for a certain sum of money, but announced that he had sold it for a lower sum than he had actually received. He quietly pocketed the difference, having given the Christian community the impression that all the money had gone to them. Sapphira may not have been in on the scheme initially, but she was well aware of what her husband had done.

When Peter discovered the corrupt situation, he confronted Ananias and Sapphira separately. When publicly faced with their deception, each fell over dead. Readers are likely to infer that the deaths of Ananias and Sapphira came as God's direct punishment for their dishonesty. Herein lies the problem.

If this is indeed a miracle of punishment, then it is the only miracle of punishment in the New Testament. And if it is a miracle of punishment, it goes against the dominant spirit and themes of Jesus' life and message: love, grace, and forgiveness. Even Simon Peter—the man who confronts Ananias and Sapphira—deliberately and publicly betrayed Jesus. Yet he had adequate time and opportunity to repent and be forgiven. How, then, should we interpret this troubling situation?

We must understand that Luke wrote the Acts of the Apostles approximately fifty years after this event occurred in Jerusalem. He wrote to a Gentile Christian community in a locale and culture far removed from Jerusalem. The historical source of his information was either a spoken tradition that had been passed down for half a century, or a short written account that had more recently preserved the older spoken tradition.

Based on Luke's sources, we can assume three things to be true. First, a financial scandal in the early Church was brought about by Ananias and Sapphira. Second, shortly after the scandal was revealed, both Ananias and Sapphira died. Third, the early Jerusalem Christians were stunned by the coinciding deaths, and some directly attributed their demise to their sinful actions. However, the story as received—and then written—by the writer of Acts was likely exaggerated over time in terms of its harsh, punitive tone, as well as the dramatic role that Peter plays as "public executioner." This is the majority view of current New Testament scholars, and it is my opinion as well.

With those facts as background, let us move beyond the thorny and debatable aspects of the story and instead focus on the deeper meaning, which is firm and clear. Christian disciples today can learn much from this ancient tragedy.

The Sin of Ananias

What was the sin of Ananias? We could call his sin embezzlement, but this term is too severe. If Ananias did embezzle, at least he embezzled his own money. The central issue of his sin is a simple one: *Ananias did not do what he had publicly committed to do.*

The power of this story is that once Ananias's sin is defined, the words fly off the page and hit us in the face. We realize that each of us has committed the sin of Ananias. As Christians we all have failed to do what we have publicly committed to do.

Let's look at one glaring example. When we become Christians, we commit ourselves to living as Jesus lived. Jesus was a devout Jew. He believed in tithing his income, as the Jewish scripture commanded. Jesus stated clearly, "Render to Caesar the things that are Caesar's and to God the things that are God's" (Matthew 22:21). It would be difficult to make a case that Jesus did not tithe his income unto God.

Growing up in the Baptist tradition, I decided to become a Christian when I was eight years old. Soon after I was baptized, I remember my parents sitting down with me one night and teaching me that the Bible instructs that I should tithe my financial income. My allowance had recently been increased to the grand sum of fifty cents. They helped me understand that as a new Christian, I was to place a nickel in the offering plate every Sunday.

My fledgling financial commitment did not last long. Even an eight-year-old soon realizes that there is seldom enough money to make it through the week. Something had to give. So, I gave up tithing.

Our sins, however, do find us out. When I was twenty-three, I married my wife, Beth. I remember the first Sunday of our married life. We had just moved into married housing on the campus of the Southern Baptist Theological Seminary in Louisville, Kentucky. The day before, I had made our first rent payment, and now we were flat broke. Thinking of this sobering fact as I tied my tie and dressed for church, I heard my new bride's voice, "Honey, have you written our check for the offering plate?" Suddenly the knot of my tie grew tighter!

The truth was that I had not tithed to God since I had pledged a nickel as an eight-year-old. But this was not the case for Beth. She is made of more authentic stuff. Since her childhood she had taken tithing seriously and she explained to me that we—meaning "I"—would too. I was too stunned to protest and too newly wed to have the courage of no convictions. As a result, for the last twenty-eight years, we have tithed our income. Beth—more so than God—made a committed tither out of me. And I have learned to be grateful! Indeed, I have discovered that tithing is one of the most meaningful and rewarding spiritual disciplines in my life.

On the surface, the sin of Ananias—and the sin of young Scott Walker—does not seem like a capital offense. We all make public commitments that we do not honor. Such intentional neglect on our part hardly seems like a sin that could lead to death. However, consider for a moment that if all Christians fulfilled their tithing commitment, millions who starve each year could be fed, the homeless sheltered, the naked clothed, and the oppressed set free (see Luke 4:16-20). People do die because Christians do not keep their commitments.

But there is another level to this truth. Something spiritual dies within us when we commit the sin of Ananias. When I don't allow my commitment to Christ to be the highest priority in my life, my spiritual vitality declines. When I don't discipline myself to love, care, pray, meditate, worship, tithe, and share with others, I grow increasingly unhealthy.

Centuries ago a public scandal took place within the early Christian Church that demanded a major decision. This decision would set direction and establish precedent for the future of Christendom. The decision centered on the issue of whether it is all right to say one thing publicly and do another thing privately. Peter correctly confronted the situation, and said, in effect, "Let your word be your bond." For when we do not honor what we have pledged to give to God, disease and death are the result.

The Sin of Sapphira

Sapphira obviously had little in common with my wife! When Ananias announced that he was watering down his gift to God, Sapphira may not have agreed, but she certainly did not object. She simply let things roll along. Sapphira's sin was *the sin of passive complacency.* This too has always been a sin among Christians.

Ambrose Bierce was a great American satirist of the nineteenth century. He wrote *The Devil's Dictionary,* which is a treasure box of wisdom laced with humor. Recently I came across Bierce's definition for the word *Occident:*

> Occident, n. The part of the world lying west (or east) of the Orient. It is largely inhabited by Christians, a powerful sub-tribe of the Hypocrites, whose principal industries are murder and cheating, which they are pleased to call "war" and "commerce." These, also, are the principal industries of the Orient.[2]

These words are a hundred years old. But the satiric truth could have been written two thousand years ago or today. Since the days of Sapphira, Christians have often been seen as a "powerful sub-tribe of the Hypocrites," because we passively condone much evil.

Each day that I drive to my church office, I pass by neighborhoods that are filled with old, dilapidated houses occupied by people who work hard but are barely making a living. Scarcely able to afford food and clothe their children, they do not have the financial means to winterize their homes or to buy an air conditioner during the dangerous heat of summer. Ironically, these islands of poverty are encircled by three hundred Christian churches in our community. But few Christian congregations are doing anything to significantly help the plight of the poor. We passively watch while the evil causes of poverty devour God's children. We withhold our money, our influence, and our spiritual energy from making a difference in our own communities.

Whether we commit an evil deed (Ananias) or condone an evil deed (Sapphira), we hurt the kingdom of God. This was the crisis that Peter confronted. He realized that the combination of those two traits makes for a deadly marriage.

And the Young Men Came and Buried Them . . .

It is important to note who in this story takes away the bodies of Ananias and Sapphira for burial. It is a younger, impressionable generation. Herein is symbolic truth that should not be missed.

The young are the most perceptive about the presence of evil and hypocrisy. As Leo Tolstoy wrote in his epic novel *Anna Karenina,* "Hypocrisy in anything whatever may deceive the cleverest and most penetrating man, but the least wide-awake of children recognizes it, and is revolted by it, however ingeniously it may be disguised."[3] The great danger caused by hypocrisy and complacency among Christians is that our own children will recognize it, and will walk away from Christian faith and participation within the Christian community.

Many times I have been revolted by things I have seen and experienced among Christians. But many Christians I have known were and are true to their faith and consistent in its practice. Many of those who have guided me (and I believe they are saints) have made their share of mistakes. They had their faults and their sins to confess and resolve. However, there was a resounding authenticity to their quest and desire to follow Jesus.

[handwritten margin note: not hypocrites]

What every emerging generation must experience within the Church is not so much perfection and orderly lives. Rather, it is to see adults who sincerely strive to be what they have professed to be, and who do not sit passively by and let evil reign in the world.

As I conclude this chapter, I reflect on the tragic life of the nineteenth-century philosopher Friedrich Nietzsche. Nietzsche was born in Prussia in 1844. Both of his grandfathers and his father were Christian pastors. His father died when Friedrich was five years old, leaving his son without a strong male presence in his life.

Friedrich grew up in the Christian Church. He also attended excellent schools. However, as he grew older, he became disenchanted with Christianity and the Church. A brilliant and sensitive young man, he saw much among his fellow Christians that he felt was hypocritical. Caustic by nature, he summarized his adolescent feelings by writing, "These Christians must show me they are redeemed before I will believe in their redeemer."[4] In his reflections on the Church, Nietzsche's emerging voice is also heard through one of his fictional characters, a madman, who exclaims, "What are these churches now if they are not the tombs and sepulchers of God?"[5]

Cut loose from his moorings of faith, Nietzsche, at the young age of twenty-four, became a professor of classical philology at the University of Basel. He soon became famous for espousing the view that God is dead—that a belief in God cannot be credible within the context of emerging modern knowledge and the sham of cultural Christian religion. As Nietzsche wrote: "God is dead. God remains dead. And we have killed him. How shall we, murderers of all murderers, console ourselves?"[6]

Nietzsche saw such consolation in the emergence of a new set of values that he perceived as "faithful to the earth." From these modern values would come the birth of a race of Overmen or Supermen.

Not too many years after declaring God to be dead, Nietzsche experienced a total psychic breakdown from which he never recovered. Upon his death in 1900, his sister, Elisabeth, collected many of his unpublished notes and essays, At the same time, Elisabeth became increasingly involved in the growing anti-Semitic movement in Germany. She tailored her brother's writings to strengthen her philosophic views.

In one of the great ironies of history, the young Adolf Hitler became enamored with Nietzsche's writings and concepts. They formed a philosophical cornerstone for Hitler's twisted worldview and his desire to produce the super-race. The catastrophic result was a world cast into world war and the loss of millions of lives. Such tragedy was birthed when an impressionable young man named Friedrich Nietzsche, the product of generations of Christian pastors, could not find credibility of faith or authentic example within the Christian community of his childhood.

Death is the price of Christian hypocrisy and passive complacency in the face of evil. This is what the episode of Ananias and Sapphira taught the earliest Christians. And the lesson of this story applies equally to our lives today. Christian disciples must earnestly seek to be true to their public professions of faith.

Reflections
Matthew 6:1-4, 24; 23:25-28

What you are thunders so loud, I can't hear what you say.
  —*Ralph Waldo Emerson*[7]

It is easier to fight for one's principles than to live up to them.
  —*Alfred Adler*[8]

Infidelity does not consist in believing or in disbelieving; it consists in professing to believe what he does not believe.
  —*Thomas Paine*[9]

We do not so much break the laws of God as we break ourselves upon them.
  —*Paul Tillich*[10]

Dear Father,
  I would have preferred to skip this story of Ananias and Sapphira. My excuse would be the complexity of the literary critique and interpretation. But the real reason, O Lord, is that when I read this story, I must come to terms with myself.

I confess that at times I am a hypocrite, professing one thing and doing another. And you, O Lord, know that I shy away from conflict. It is hard for me to confront what I know to be wrong in the world around me. I am well acquainted with the ways of Ananias and Sapphira. And their spirit is killing my soul.

Father, enable me to be true to my convictions. Give me the courage to stand tall in a world where we are told to sit down and be silent. Amen.

Questions among Friends

1. Give an illustration or example of the sin of Ananias—of not doing something that you have publicly professed to do. The illustration can derive from your own life or the life of someone else. Also, give an illustration of the sin of Sapphira—passive complacency in the face of evil.

2. Discuss your views of Christian financial stewardship. What do you think about the spiritual discipline of tithing?

3. Share the story of a time when you were personally hurt or affected by Christian hypocrisy.

4. What impact has reflection on the story of Ananias and Sapphira had on you?

Chapter Seventeen

TEARING DOWN WALLS

Peter went up on the housetop about the sixth hour to pray. But he became hungry and was desiring to eat; but while they were making preparations, he fell into a trance; and he saw the sky opened up, and an object like a great sheet coming down, lowered by four corners to the ground, and there were in it all kinds of four-footed animals and crawling creatures of the earth and birds of the air. A voice came to him, "Get up, Peter, kill and eat!" But Peter said, "By no means, Lord, for I have never eaten anything unholy and unclean." Again a voice came to him a second time, "What God has cleansed, no longer consider unholy." This happened three times, and immediately the object was taken up into the sky. . . .

Opening his mouth, Peter said:

"I most certainly understand now that God is not one to show partiality, but in every nation the man who fears Him and does what is right is welcome to Him." (Acts 10:9-16, 34-35)

THE TENTH CHAPTER OF ACTS RELATES ONE OF THE MOST INTERESTING and important stories in the New Testament, a story that shaped and defined the future of Christianity. This story centers around an encounter between two very different men, Peter and Cornelius. Let's focus first on Cornelius.

Cornelius was a Roman citizen and a centurion in the Roman army. As a centurion, he held the highest rank of a noncommissioned officer, roughly equivalent to a sergeant major in the American Army. Though centurions did not hold commissions from the Roman Senate, they were appointed by the emperor.

The basic unit of the Roman army was a legion, comprising six thousand men. Sixty centurions were assigned to a legion, and each centurion commanded one hundred men. The centurion was the most essential link in the chain of command of the Roman army. Centurions were the tough and tried veterans who held the ranks together. Thus, Cornelius was a man of honor, experience, and ability.

As this story opens, Cornelius is assigned to the Italian cohort (six hundred troops) stationed at Caesarea, located on the Mediterranean Sea, seven miles northwest of Jerusalem. It was originally a small Phoenician anchorage, but Herod the Great had built a new city on the old site and named it Caesarea Maritima, in honor of Caesar Augustus. Recent excavations show the city to have been beautiful and elaborate. Caesarea was the home of the Roman procurators, such as Pilate, who traveled to Jerusalem only for Jewish feast days, so they could keep order during such unstable times. It is likely that the Italian cohort was assigned to protect the Roman procurator.

Evidently Cornelius had been in Israel long enough to be influenced by Jewish culture. We are told that he was a God Fearer, which meant that he had come to accept the Jewish religious faith as his own, but had stopped short of becoming a full-fledged Jew. In order to become a Jew, he would have to be physically circumcised, make donations to the Temple in Jerusalem, undergo baptism by immersion, and practice Jewish dietary laws. Being a Roman soldier, it was more practical for Cornelius to worship the Jewish God without becoming Jewish. Thus, in the eyes of Jews, Cornelius remained a Gentile.

Now let's look at Simon Peter. Peter was a Jew by birth and a Jew by conviction. Though he was devout, he was not as strict as a Pharisee in keeping the Law. In Acts 10:14, for instance, Peter states that he has never eaten anything that was not prescribed by Jewish Law. It is also noted that Peter had been staying with Simon the tanner for many days (Acts 9:43). According to Jewish Law, Simon was considered to be ritually unclean because he worked with the carcasses and skins of dead animals. A truly strict and zealous Jew would not have entered the house of such an unclean person. Thus, Peter is a faithful Jew, but he is not obsessed with keeping every jot and tittle of the Law.

With this as background, Luke brings us to witness a pivotal day, when the lives of Peter and Cornelius converged. It seems that at about three o'clock in the afternoon, Cornelius received a vision. In the vision an angel of God instructed him to "dispatch some men to Joppa and send for a man named Simon, who is also called Peter" (Acts 10:1-5). Cornelius immediately obeyed, and sent "two of his servants and a devout soldier" on a thirty-mile journey to Joppa to find Peter (v. 7).

The next day at noon, as Cornelius's delegation neared the outskirts of Joppa, an unsuspecting Peter climbed to the rooftop porch of Simon the tanner's house to pray and rest while lunch was being prepared. Peter too received a vision. He saw the sky open up and "a great sheet coming down, lowered by four corners to the ground." Inside the sheet were all the various animals, birds, and seafood that devout Jews were forbidden to eat. Then Peter heard the voice of God say, "Get up, Peter, kill and eat!" Peter immediately protested in his sleep, but the vision was repeated two more times. Then

Peter awoke, totally perplexed by the meaning of the vision, only to hear the delegation from Cornelius calling at the front gate. Stunned, he greeted them, invited them to lunch, and they spent the night. After much conversation Peter agreed to return with them to Caesarea to talk with Cornelius (Acts 10:9-23).

When Peter and Cornelius finally met in Caesarea several days later, they discovered that they had both received visions and that the visions were related. Cornelius gathered his family and friends together, and Peter shared with them how Jesus of Nazareth was the fulfillment of the ancient Jewish prophecy that God would send his Messiah to Israel. Peter told them of Jesus' life, teaching, death, and resurrection. Then an unexpected thing happened: "While Peter was still speaking these words, the Holy Spirit fell upon all those who were listening to the message. All the circumcised believers who came with Peter were amazed, because the gift of the Holy Spirit had been poured out on the Gentiles also. For they were hearing them speaking with tongues and exalting God" (Acts 10:44-46).

Peter was stunned to see Gentiles manifesting the spiritual gifts of the Holy Spirit, but he could not deny that the Spirit of God was acting in their midst. Peter concluded, "Surely no one can refuse the water for these to be baptized who have received the Holy Spirit just as we did, can he?" (Acts 10:47). Peter then directed that Cornelius, his family, and his friends be baptized.

In this dramatic story, Simon Peter's entire worldview and value system were shaken and revised. What did Peter learn through this pivotal moment in Christian history?

One in Christ

In a dramatic way, the Spirit of God grasped a culturally biased Simon Peter by the scruff of his Jewish neck and shook him. Wide-eyed, Peter instantly understood that all people are equally God's children. As Peter concluded, "I most certainly understand now that God is not one to show partiality, but in every nation the man who fears Him and does what is right is welcome to Him."

The Apostle Paul—Pharisee that he used to be—came to the same understanding. Broadening the scope of Peter's words, Paul writes to Christians in Galatia: "For you are all sons of God through faith in Christ Jesus. For all of you who were baptized into Christ have clothed yourselves with Christ. There is neither Jew nor Greek, there is neither slave nor free man, there is neither male nor female; for you are all one in Christ Jesus. And if you belong to Christ, then you are Abraham's descendants, heirs according to promise (Galatians 3:26-29).

The writer of the Gospel of John also recognized this truth. In perhaps the most well-known passage of the New Testament, John states, "For God so loved the world, that He gave His only begotten Son, *that whoever believes in Him* shall not perish, but have eternal life (John 3:16, my emphasis). Salvation and Christian community are open to every person.

Peter came to see that the Gospel of Jesus Christ is radically inclusive. There is a fundamental equality within the Christian community; nationality, race, gender, and social status have no bearing in it. We are all "in Christ."

During my last year in seminary, I studied the Acts of the Apostles with Dr. Jon Polhill. On the first day of class, Dr. Polhill said to us: "We are not going to begin our study today by turning to the first verse in Acts. Rather, we will begin by reading the very last verses in Acts." Then he asked his students to read in unison Acts 28:30-31: "And [Paul] stayed two full years in his own rented quarters and was welcoming all who came to him, preaching the kingdom of God and teaching concerning the Lord Jesus Christ with all openness, unhindered."

As the echo of our voices faded, Dr. Polhill continued: "You will never understand Luke's central message in Acts if you do not underline and highlight the last word—*unhindered.* This word is the key to unlocking the meaning of this book. The Acts of the Apostles is the story of how Christianity moved from being a faith limited and shackled by the confines of Jewish legalism to being a universal faith open to all people and all cultures. It is the story of how Christianity became an *unhindered* gospel!"

I have never forgotten Dr. Polhill's words. And every time my thoughts are distorted by my own cultural biases, racial bigotry, gender prejudice, and parochial American viewpoints, I hear again the voice of Dr. Polhill: "The word *unhindered* is the key!"

God has a way of challenging and contesting the views of each of us, and giving us a new vision of how we must live and act. Sometimes such confrontation awakens us from a deep sleep and changes our world. It broadens our minds and challenges old thought patterns. The God of creation is still forming us, chipping away at the biases that hinder us from building friendships and loving others.

Walls of Insignificance

Through his encounter with Cornelius, Peter also learned that some of the things Christians count as important—and which separate and alienate us from others—are really quite insignificant. I remember when, as a teenager, this truth struck me forcefully. I was sitting in a theater in small-town, rural

Georgia, munching popcorn and watching the movie adaptation of James Michener's novel *Hawaii*. In this classic story, American Christian missionaries from Puritan New England arrive on the shores of Hawaii and determine to persuade the Hawaiians to become Christians. At first the Hawaiians responded well to the missionaries' overtures of love and friendship. They even began to accept Christianity. But then comes the scene in which the missionaries instruct the Hawaiians to dress like the missionaries. The women are to cover their bare breasts with blouses, their heads with bonnets, and the men are to wear wool pants and coats. Suddenly a cultural wall was erected between pious Puritans and native Hawaiians. Quickly relationships deteriorated, and friendships grew strained. Any further ability to authentically share the essence of Christianity was undermined by stressing what was insignificant—a New England dress code!

Sitting in the darkness, I realized that so much of what I had been taught as a Christian is not truly "Christian" as much as it is American or Western or European. As the movie ended and the house lights rose, I looked around to realize that American southern culture of the 1960s mandated that white people watch movies from the ground floor and that black people be relegated to the balcony. I reflected that my own home church would not allow a black American to worship in our sanctuary. Suddenly I realized that I was no better than the old Puritan missionaries who were distorting the Gospel in Hawaii. I was passively allowing racial prejudice to erect walls of separation in my own hometown. I was enabling things of insignificance— the color of a person's skin—to become barriers to friendship and Christian influence.

One of the biggest dangers among American Christians is that we often fail to separate American culture from Christian values. And there is frequently a world of difference. It is the cultural trappings of our faith that alienate others who are both inside and outside of Christian fellowship. We erect walls of insignificance.

Tearing Down Walls

Robert Frost is one of my favorite poets. Frost was a man of the earth. In his early adult years, he often toiled as a farmer, writing poetry late at night by lantern light. His experiences in a New England agrarian setting deeply shaped his thought and poetic gift.

One night, following a day of mending stone walls, Frost began to compose one of his best-loved poems, "Mending Wall." Reflecting on moments spent inspecting his property lines with his adjoining neighbor, he writes:

Something there is that doesn't love a wall,

That spends the frozen-ground-swell under it
And spills the upper boulders in the sun,
And makes gaps even two can pass abreast. . . .

I let my neighbor know beyond the hill;
And on a day we meet to walk the line
And set the wall between us once again.
We keep the wall between us as we go. . . .

He is all pine and I am apple orchard.
My apple trees will never get across
And eat the cones under his pines, I tell him.
He only says, "Good fences make good neighbors."
Spring is the mischief in me, and I wonder
If I could put a notion in his head:
"Why do they make good neighbors? Isn't it
Where there are cows? But here there are no cows.
Before I built a wall I'd ask to know
What I was walling in or walling out,
And to whom I was like to give offense.
Something there is that doesn't love a wall,
That wants it down." I could say "Elves" to him,
But it's not elves exactly, and I'd rather
He said it for himself. I see him there,
Bringing a stone grasped firmly by the top
In each hand, like an old-stone savage armed.
He moves in darkness as it seems to me,
Not of woods only and the shade of trees.
He will not go behind his father's saying,
And he likes having thought of it so well
He says again, "Good fences make good neighbors."[1]

In simple yet profound language, Frost states, "Something there is that doesn't love a wall, that wants it down." That "something," I believe, is the *image of God* created within us! Yet it is the traditionalists—those of us who are like an "old-stone savage armed"—who will not question cultural customs and refuse to "go behind [our] father's saying." We insist on erecting stone barriers without asking, "What am I walling in or walling out?" And the result, as Frost knew well, is not so much good neighbors as distant neighbors.

I believe that it is the Spirit of God who is about the business of tearing down walls, who "makes gaps even two can pass abreast." It is the Spirit of God who is moving to make the gospel an unhindered gospel. God will continue to disturb our sleep and our waking moments with visions of how life should be. He will show us that what we have been taught is not always right. He will cause us to question what builds up walls, and to yearn for what creates doors and windows into the lives and depths of one another.

As I conclude this chapter, I vividly remember a moment several months ago when my wife and I were visiting St. Petersburg, Russia. We were traveling with some Baptist Christians from Texas who were studying the plight of street children and orphans in Russia. On Sunday morning we all decided to attend a Russian Baptist church.

As we entered the beautiful church, its sanctuary crowded to overflowing, we were not aware that this Baptist congregation was observing communion that Sunday. Ushered to the front of the church, we were seated next to the choir. Within moments we Americans were captivated by the moving service. The choral anthems were beautiful, and the sermon—translated into English—deeply moved me. Then it was time for communion.

As the deacons moved to stand in front of the altar, large goblets of wine were uncovered on the communion table, and the largest loaves of bread I had ever seen were broken into small pieces. Then my friend sitting next to me whispered: "Scott, this church probably practices closed communion. Only the members of this specific church can partake. So don't look disappointed."

Well, I was disappointed. For the last hour, I had been enthralled in sharing worship with Christians in a nation that had been at political odds with my country for decades. But political walls had been literally torn down and hands of friendship extended between Russia and the United States. I deeply yearned to share in the fellowship of communion with these Russian Christians.

As the elements were distributed among the congregation by the deacons, I saw a handsome, middle-aged deacon moving toward us Americans. Suddenly he stopped, with a look of confusion and concern on his face. I could tell that he did not know what to do. Should he serve the American Christians bread and wine, or should he move on? For a moment he stood transfixed, and then he anxiously looked toward the pastor. The old Russian pastor's face broke into a smile, and he nodded his head in affirmation. The deacon's frozen face beamed, and with joy he came to serve us communion. As I ate the bread and drank the wine, tears ran down my face—as they are right now as I write these words months later. I could hear the stones of age-old walls toppling to the ground. I could see gates in cultural walls swing open on rusted hinges to allow two to pass abreast. Though there was no speaking in tongues, flashes of fire, or the rush of wind from the wings of God's Spirit, it still felt like Pentecost to me. It was a God-gifted moment I will never forget.

YEARS AGO SIMON PETER WAS SURPRISED TO LEARN THAT GOD IS always inclusive, not exclusive. He gleaned from a vision that Christianity soars above every nation, race, gender, and creed. In a brief moment, he glimpsed that Christianity is universal truth meant for all people and that the message of Jesus Christ cannot be hindered by the stone walls of prejudice, bias, and cultural shortsightedness. Followers of Christ must be good neighbors to everyone.

Reflections

Malachi 2:10; Matthew 7:12, 28:20; 1 Corinthians 12:12-13; Colossians 3:11; 1 Peter 2:17; Revelation 7:9-10

If I perceive in another person mainly the surface, I perceive mainly the difference. If I penetrate to the core, I perceive our identity, the fact of our brotherhood.
    —*Erich Fromm*[2]

Great Spirit, help me never to judge another until I have walked two weeks in his moccasins.
    —*Sioux Native American Prayer*

Tolerance implies no lack of commitment to one's own beliefs. Rather it condemns the oppression or persecution of others.
    —*John F. Kennedy*[3]

Dogs bark at a person whom they do not know.
    —*Heraclitus (500 B.C.)*[4]

Religion is as effectually destroyed by bigotry as by indifference.
    —*Ralph Waldo Emerson*[5]

The most fatal illusion is the settled point of view. Since life is growth and motion, a fixed point of view kills anybody who has one.
    —*Brooks Atkinson*[6]

Dear Father,

I must admit that I secretly harbor my share of bias and prejudice. There are some people I do not like, customs I find offensive, cultures I do not care to understand. I shy away from such people, Lord. I do not invite them into my life. Nor do I enter their world.

I often agree that good fences make good neighbors. I have grown comfortable on my side of the fence. But I know that you have called me to topple walls, flatten fences, open gates, and remove barriers to friendship.

Lord, give me a vision of how life should be in Your Kingdom. Soften my heart and give me compassion for all people. May I always extend a hand of friendship and a smile of welcome to every stranger. And may I learn to love those who are far different from me. Amen.

Questions among Friends

1. Share a time when your traditional, cultural, or Christian views were challenged, questioned, or perhaps altered. What created the confrontation? What gave you a vision for the need for change?

2. How have you struggled with prejudice in your life? How have you seen the Christian Church grapple with issues of bias, prejudice, or exclusiveness?

3. What do you consider to be some insignificant issues that have caused division, hurt, and turmoil within the Christian Church? Have these issues affected your life?

4. In what ways have Christians erected fences that keep people from entering into Christian faith and fellowship?

5. Describe a time when you saw walls of separation torn down between fellow Christians or between the Christian Church and the world.

6. What wall of separation do you wish you could topple today? What steps might you take to topple it?

Chapter Eighteen

"AND HE . . . WENT TO ANOTHER PLACE . . ."

Now about that time Herod the king laid hands on some who belonged to the church in order to mistreat them. And he had James the brother of John put to death with a sword. When he saw that it pleased the Jews, he proceeded to arrest Peter also. Now it was during the days of Unleavened Bread. When he had seized him, he put him in prison, delivering him to four squads of soldiers to guard him, intending after the Passover to bring him out before the people. So Peter was kept in the prison, but prayer for him was being made fervently by the church to God.

On the very night when Herod was about to bring him forward, Peter was sleeping between two soldiers, bound with two chains, and guards in front of the door were watching over the prison. And behold, an angel of the Lord suddenly appeared and a light shone in the cell; and he struck Peter's side and woke him saying, "Get up quickly." And his chains fell off his hands. And the angel said to him, "Gird yourself and put on your sandals." And he did so. And he said to him, "Wrap your cloak around you and follow me." And He went out and continued to follow, and he did not know that what was being done by the angel was real, but thought he was seeing a vision. When they had passed the first and second guard, they came to the iron gate that leads into the city, which opened for them by itself; and they went out and went along one street, and immediately the angel departed from him. When Peter came to himself, he said, "Now I know for sure that the Lord has sent forth His angel and rescued me from the hand of Herod and from all that the Jewish people were expecting." And when he realized this, he went to the house of Mary, the mother of John who was also called Mark, where many were gathered together and were praying. When he knocked at the door of the gate, a servant-girl named Rhoda came to answer. When she recognized Peter's voice, because of her joy she did not open the gate, but ran in and announced that Peter was standing in front of the gate. They said to her, "You are out of your mind!" But she kept insisting that it was so. They kept saying, "It is his angel." But Peter continued knocking; and when they had opened the door, they saw him and were amazed. But motioning to them with his hand to be silent, he described to them how the Lord had led him out of the prison. And he said, "Report these things to James and the brethren." Then he left and went to another place. (Acts 12:1-17)

THE YEAR WAS A.D. 44, AND FOURTEEN YEARS HAD PASSED SINCE THE death and resurrection of Jesus. Pontius Pilate had been recalled to Rome, and Herod Antipas—who mocked Jesus at his trial and beheaded John the Baptist—was dead. Herod Agrippa ruled, and in five short years had consolidated as much territory as his famous grandfather, Herod the Great, had governed. Herod Agrippa was ruthless and confident of political success.

During the course of these same fourteen years, Simon Peter emerged as the leader of the Christian community in Jerusalem. Recently, however, Herod Agrippa decided to rid Israel of Jewish Christians. For reasons unknown, he first arrested James, the son of Zebedee, and executed him. Then, perceiving that this action was popular, Herod Agrippa arrested and imprisoned Simon Peter.

As the present scene opens, it is late at night, and Peter is guarded by a quaternion of soldiers. A quaternion was four soldiers who guarded a prisoner for six hours. Then they were replaced by a fresh quaternion. Each of Peter's wrists was chained to the arm of a soldier, while two other soldiers guarded the prison cell door. Should a prisoner escape, the quaternion would be executed. In an ancient world, this was maximum security.

Peter was arrested just before the Feast of Unleavened Bread. The Passover was on the fourteenth day of Nisan. To commemorate the hurried escape of the ancient Hebrews from Egypt, the Jews could not eat leavened bread on the Passover and for seven days following it. During this Feast of Unleavened Bread, government functions recessed and no trial or execution could take place.

The irony of the timing of his arrest could not have escaped Peter. Fourteen years before, Jesus of Nazareth had been arrested and hastily executed in Jerusalem as Passover was dawning. Now, in this same holy season, Peter was facing his own trial.

This did not happen, however. Peter was miraculously rescued by the power of God. The specific circumstances of the escape were not clear even to Peter. It seemed to him like a dream, a surreal experience. But when a groggy Simon Peter awoke, he was standing in the street outside the prison with vague recollections of a bright light, an angel, chains being released, and doors swinging open. With his heart in his throat, Peter ran for his life, seeking a place of safety.

A God of Deliverance

What can we learn from Simon Peter's dramatic escape from prison? First, it is clear throughout biblical history that God is characterized by the word *deliverance*. During the very week the Jews celebrated God's stunning rescue of their ancestors from Egypt twelve hundred years before, Simon Peter was liberated from prison by God's power. Fourteen years prior to Peter's escape, Jesus of Nazareth was also captured by death and imprisoned in a tomb. Yet God delivered him through the miracle of *resurrection*. The Bible is emphatic that God is a God of deliverance.

What do I mean by deliverance? Many times we are constrained by events or circumstances from which we have no power to escape, conquer, control, or be released. Both of our wrists are chained to armed guards, and our prison cell is bolted shut. We seem to have no option but to wither away in captivity or to die. Then we suddenly discover a power beyond us. We are rescued by events beyond our ability or imagination.

We can find many examples of such bondage; one of the clearest is the captivating force of addiction. Good men and women are imprisoned by multiple forms of addiction: substance abuse, pornography, compulsive shopping, gambling, workaholism, perfectionism, power trips, and eating disorders, to name only a few. My maternal grandfather was such an addict. Try as he might, he could not break loose from alcohol's control of his life. He died in a drunken stupor.

The one technique that has helped countless addicts overcome their addictions is an approach popularly known as the Twelve Steps program. By slowly working together through twelve consecutive steps of recovery, many addicts are released from bondage. Listen to the first three steps on which this healing program is based:

> Step One: We admitted we were powerless over alcohol [or other addictions] and that our lives had become unmanageable.
> Step Two: We came to believe that a Power greater than ourselves could restore us to sanity.
> Step Three: We made a decision to turn our will and our lives over to the care of God as we understood Him.

What thousands of addicts have discovered is that there is no escape from the most notorious prisons unless the power of God—not our own strength—releases us from bondage. And God is able to conquer all evil powers, even the greatest of addictions—sin—and the inevitable prison of death.

When Peter awoke a free man, he was sure of one thing: he had done nothing to release himself. It was the power of God that broke chains, subdued guards, unlocked doors, and swung open gates. God is a God of deliverance.

A God of Perfect Timing

God is also a God of perfect timing. He does not always deliver us when we want him to. But he is always faithful to deliver us *in the fullness of time.*

I am sure that several generations of Hebrews who were enslaved in Egypt prayed for release, before God used Moses to liberate his people from Pharaoh. Jesus fervently prayed that God would free him from facing the torture of crucifixion. Still, he was crucified. Peter probably gave up hope that his prayers for freedom would be answered. Yet, at the right time—in the fullness of time—God did provide deliverance for Peter and Jesus and the ancient Hebrews.

I remember a time as a young adult when I was greatly frustrated by the aspect of timing and deliverance. For five wonderful years, I had been an associate pastor at the First Baptist Church of Athens, Georgia, and was coming to the completion of my doctoral studies at the University of Georgia. In short, I was ready to move on. I was tired of graduate school, I felt that I had "grown through" my apprenticeship as an associate pastor, and I was eager to be the pastor of a church. In my own perception of life's rhythm, a pastor search committee should have been knocking on my door.

Well, no knocks came, and I was champing at the bit. As I sat in the worship service one Sunday morning, silently reminding God how he was forgetting about his "humble servant," Dr. J. W. Fanning, a retired vice-president of the University of Georgia and a patriarch of our church, walked to the pulpit to lead the morning prayer. I had grown to greatly love and appreciate this man and regard him with respect. As he bowed his head to pray, I found myself absorbed in his words. And then he said something that almost knocked me out of my chair: "God, you do not always come to us when we want you to, but you are always on time." A word from God thundered toward me through the lips of Dr. Fanning.

What God was saying to me on that day—and has reminded me of many times since then—is that my perception of timing in my life and God's perception of timing for my life are not always the same. But God is always right. God is always "on time."

Perhaps Peter needed some days to stare at a prison wall and contemplate the brevity of life before he was ready to enter the next chapter of his Christian pilgrimage. All speculation aside, we may never know the reason behind God's timing and action. But we *can* be sure that God controls the timing in our universe, our world, and even in our individual lives. He always delivers us from bondage when the time is right. Our task is to have faith that he will respond to our needs and guide our decisions in the fullness of his time—the right time.

A God of Faithfulness

When Peter awoke to find himself free and outside the prison, he immediately sought a place of safety. He ran to "the house of Mary, the mother of John who was also called Mark, where many were gathered together and were praying." As he frantically knocked on the door, a servant girl named Rhoda looked through the safety slot, saw Peter, recognized his voice, and promptly panicked. She ran inside to tell those who were praying for Peter's release that he was standing outside the door. So confident of the power of prayer were these Christians that they immediately responded, "You are out of your mind! . . . It is his angel!" Finally, they found the courage to open the door and let the poor fugitive inside.

Perhaps no more comical situation is found in the New Testament than this scene—a room full of Christians praying specifically for Peter's release and yet adamant in their belief that such escape was not possible. But I have to admit that I often pray without believing that a significant change can transpire in my life. This is true particularly when I have prayed for many months and years for a specific problem to be rectified, and yet the situation remains the same.

Perhaps the lesson we must learn from this scene sounds odd—even heretical—on first hearing. This lesson is the simple fact that God's faithfulness is not dependent on our faithfulness, that God's ability to act is not dependent on our ability to believe, and that God can release prisoners from bondage even when we are filled with doubt and despair. I am not saying that God is not aided by our prayers and attitudes of faithfulness; I am certain he is. But God is not limited by our human frailty. God is motivated only by love, and will not be bound by our human weakness. For God raised Jesus from the dead when not a single disciple expected it, anticipated it, hoped for it, or prayed for it. God is a God who surprises us with joy, even in the midst of doubt, cynicism, and disbelief. He takes the ghostlike wisps of dying faith and transforms them into the warm-blooded presence of belief.

A God of Guidance

After Peter told the Christians at Mary's house the details of his escape, the writer of Acts concludes, "And [Peter] said, 'Report these things to James and the brethren.' Then he left and went to another place." With these brief words, Peter walks off the stage of the New Testament, never to be seen in the spotlight again. We are simply told, "He left and went to another place."

Simon Peter did, however, leave a few footprints for us to follow. Knowing that his life was endangered in Israel, Peter and his wife fled their native land to become itinerant missionaries to Jewish Christians in other parts of the Mediterranean world. Paul relates that Peter took his "believing wife" and ministered in Corinth and in Antioch.[1] Finally, we know that Peter ended up in Rome, where he gave strong leadership to Christians in this imperial city. In advanced age he was martyred in the Neronian persecution, and—if early Christian tradition is true—he was crucified upside down on a cross.[2]

How could a simple, rustic fisherman from Galilee end up in the imperial city of Rome? How could a man who blatantly betrayed Christ and shouted, "I don't know this man!" live to be remembered as the Prince of the Apostles? How could a man so full of weakness and failure become the representative figure of Christian discipleship in the writing of the first Gospel, the Gospel of Mark? The answer, of course, is, "Only by the power and grace of God." Herein is hope for us all!

When we accept the invitation to follow Jesus and set out on our journey of faith, we can never know where life will take us. As the Good Shepherd guides us down our path, he uses our mistakes—perhaps even more than our victories—to teach us spiritual lessons. Slowly we learn to be more like Jesus. And as the Spirit of God shapes us, we are asked to take on greater roles of leadership.

Ultimately we learn that God is a God of deliverance. He delivers us from ourselves and from self-destruction. We discover that God is a God of faithfulness, for he never gives up on us or revokes his blessing. But above all, we come to know that God is a God of love. And it is God's love that carves away at the rock—the Petros—of our being and slowly creates a masterpiece.

As we conclude this study of the life of Peter, I am thankful for this very human man—this humble fisherman—who gives me hope that I too can be a disciple of Jesus'. Above the surge of the Galilean Sea, I hear again Jesus say, "Come, follow Me!"

Reflections
Exodus 6:6, Psalm 37:5-7, Ecclesiastes 3:1, Isaiah 41:9-10, Galatians 4:3-5

The idea that God's providence means that he looks after those who serve him by a special use of his power in terms of favoritism is an immoral idea and insulting to both man and God. No true Christian wants to opt out of the trials that beset others, and no worthy idea of God could include his establishment of a kind of insurance scheme by which, if God be worshiped, cancer, for example, could be avoided. Jesus himself who spoke so eloquently of God's providential care, quoting the lilies and the birds, never promised a "special Providence" to his own. Rather he promised that they would face persecution beyond the normal trials of others. But he did promise that he would see them through everything and be with them to the end.

—*Leslie D. Weatherhead*[3]

It sometimes happens that God leads us by an obscure intuition which makes us go to a particular place without our knowing what awaits us there. It sometimes happens, too, that he leads us by means of events that seem to have no religious significance. There is no such thing as chance.

—*Paul Tournier*[4]

My Lord God, I have no idea where I am going. I do not see the road ahead of me. I cannot know for certain where it will end. Nor do I really know myself, and the fact that I think I am following Your will does not mean that I am actually doing so. But I believe that the desire to please you does in fact please you. Amen.

—*Thomas Merton*[5]

Sweetly, Lord, have we heard Thee calling, "Come, follow me!"
And we see where Thy footprints falling, Lead us to Thee.
Footprints of Jesus that make the pathway glow;
We will follow the steps of Jesus where'er they go.
Then at last, when on high He sees us, Our journey done,
We will rest where the steps of Jesus end at His throne.
Footsteps of Jesus that make the pathway glow;
We will follow the steps of Jesus where'er they go.

—*Mary B. C. Slade*[6]

Dear Father,

Like the Apostle Peter, I am finding my way through life. You have led me to many places to attempt many things that I would never have dreamed possible. You have challenged me, taught me, humbled me, and encouraged me each step of the way. When I have failed you, you have never failed me. Rather you have used my weakness to help me grow strong. I thank you for loving me, O God.

Now, as I face the future, may I do so with the strong assurance that you walk with me. May the memory of my good friend, Simon Peter, accompany me and instruct me on the road of discipleship. May I be faithful as Peter was faithful, to the final day of my life on Earth. Amen.

Questions among Friends

1. Share a time when the power of God delivered you from a difficult situation or "prison cell" in your life.

2. Discuss a moment in your life when you felt that God's timing was all wrong. Did you later discover that "God was right on time?"

3. Have you ever had the experience of praying for something that you thought was impossible and yet your prayers were answered—perhaps in a way that you did not expect?

4. As you look back over your life, list some ways that God has led you to places and situations that you could have never envisioned earlier in your life.

5. How do you think that God may be leading you toward the next step on your road of discipleship?

6. As you have read the pages of this book, what are some of the major lessons that you have learned or reaffirmed about being a disciple of Jesus? How has this study most helped you?

Appendix

JOHN MARK'S RELATIONSHIP WITH THE APOSTLE PETER

[Peter] went to the house of Mary, the mother of John who was also called Mark, where many were gathered together and were praying. (Acts 12:12)

Only Luke is with me [Paul]. Pick up Mark and bring him with you, for he is useful to me for service. (2 Timothy 4:11)

She who is in Babylon [Rome], chosen together with you, sends you greetings, and so does my son, Mark. (1 Peter 5:13)

THE RELATIONSHIP BETWEEN JOHN MARK OF JERUSALEM, THE AUTHOR of the Gospel of Mark, and the Apostle Peter makes for an interesting story. In presenting this story, I take the position that the ancient writings of Papias, the bishop of Hierapolis (A.D. 60–130); Irenaeus, the bishop of Lyons (A.D. 130–200); and Eusebius of Caesarea (A.D. 260–340) are basically true and trustworthy.[1]

Early Years with Peter

John Mark was born into a Jewish family in the dense inner city of Jerusalem. It is likely that he was born shortly before, or immediately after, the death of Jesus. We know nothing of John Mark's father. His mother, Mary, however, was a Christian, and her spacious home was used as a meeting place for Christians (Acts 12:12).

149

Fourteen years after Jesus' death, John Mark was a gawky teenager when a crisis engulfed the Christian community in Jerusalem. In A.D. 44, Herod Agrippa arrested a group of Jewish Christians, including the Apostle James, the son of Zebedee. To test the waters of public opposition, Herod executed James by sword. When no great Jewish outcry or protest by Roman authorities arose, Herod ordered that the Apostle Peter, the recognized leader of the Jewish Christian community, also be arrested. However, by the miraculous intervention of God, Peter was able to escape from prison on the night before his trial. Running through the darkened streets of Jerusalem, Peter fled to John Mark's mother's house, interrupting a prayer meeting and causing quite a stir. It is likely that young John Mark remembered this highly charged moment for the rest of his life![2]

Knowing that he could not safely remain in Jerusalem, Peter and his wife hastily left Israel to begin a ministry to Jews scattered around the Mediterranean world. James, the brother of Jesus, then became the leader of the Jerusalem Christian community, until he was executed by the Sanhedrin in A.D. 62.[3]

Slipping quietly out of the gates of Jerusalem, Peter could not have known that twenty years later he would again find his life interwoven with the life of John Mark, Mary's wide-eyed son. This time, however, John Mark would be a mature and wizened man, and would meet Peter in the imperial city of Rome during intense crisis.

John Mark and Paul

For a moment let's change focus from the Apostle Peter to John Mark's relationship with the Apostle Paul. Nine years before Peter was exiled from Israel, around A.D. 35, Saul of Tarsus was dramatically converted to Christianity through a vision of the risen Christ while he was traveling to Damascus to arrest Christians. Following this traumatic and life-changing event, Paul (Saul) retreated to the solitude of Arabia for three years to pull his life back together again. When he finally emerged from the desert in A.D. 38, Paul returned to Jerusalem in hope of meeting with Peter and James, the brother of Jesus.[4]

Initially the Jerusalem Christians refused to associate with Paul, suspecting that he might be a "double agent" seeking to infiltrate their ranks. However, John Mark's kind and encouraging older cousin, Barnabas, befriended Paul and convinced the Jerusalem Christians to accept him. After a visit of fifteen days, Paul left Jerusalem because his life was endangered by his former Jewish colleagues and friends. Quietly he moved into the regions of Syria and Cilicia, and for ten years was a bivocational tent maker and Christian missionary.[5]

While Paul was away—and John Mark was growing from childhood into young adulthood—a curious thing happened in Antioch around A.D. 46. Gentiles began to become Christians. Until then Christianity had been seen as a sect of Judaism—that is, Christians were Jews who believed that Jesus, the Messiah of Israel, had come. Few Jewish Christians anticipated that Christianity should or would spread to the Gentiles, but Gentiles within the Christian community in Antioch were clearly showing evidence that they had been converted and filled by the Holy Spirit. Now the pivotal question arose in Jerusalem: Can these Gentiles in Antioch become legitimate Christians without first being converted to Judaism and being circumcised? This was a controversial issue that threatened to divide the broader Christian community.

Because he was a proven peacemaker, John Mark's cousin Barnabas was asked by the Christian church in Jerusalem to go to Antioch and investigate this troubling situation. On arriving he became convinced that the conversion experience of the Gentiles was authentic. Acts 11:23-25 states that Barnabas "rejoiced and began to encourage them, . . . and he left for Tarsus to look for Saul." Now, why would Barnabas seek out Paul? (Acts 11:19-26).

Barnabas had a good memory and a sure discernment of spiritual gifts. It is likely that of all the Jewish Christians he knew who could live, work, and relate effectively with both Jews and Gentiles, Paul was at the top of his list. This was due to Paul's unique background.

Though we know nothing of Paul's parents or family of origin, it is certain that Paul was a Jew, a member of the tribe of Benjamin, the son of a Pharisee, and, ironically, a Roman citizen. Paul grew up outside of Palestine in the major Greco-Roman trade city of Tarsus, in what is now south-central Turkey. His collected writings clearly reflect both a Hellenistic education and a formal rabbinic education. He was a man who intimately knew the worlds of both the Jew and the Gentile. If Christianity was to be preached to the Gentiles—and if Jews and Gentiles were to be wedded together into one Christian community—Paul's help would be invaluable. Barnabas brought Paul out of anonymity and thrust him into the bright spotlight of Christian history in the melting pot of Antioch.[6]

For nearly a year, Paul and Barnabas wrestled in Antioch with the task of liberating Christianity from the bondage of Jewish restrictions and freeing it to become a religious faith for all the world. In fact, it was in Antioch that this messianic sect of Judaism was first called "Christians," thus becoming increasingly distinct from the mother faith of Judaism in the eyes of a Gentile world.

Enter John Mark. After a year of ministry in Antioch, Paul and Barnabas departed on what is traditionally known as "Paul's first missionary journey," in A.D. 47 or 48. Using Antioch as their base, they proposed a journey to

Cyprus, then through southern Asia Minor, and back to Antioch. Barnabas decided to bring with him his teenage cousin John Mark to assist them in their ministry.[7]

All went well on the journey until they reached Perga. For reasons unknown, John Mark left Paul and Barnabas and returned home to Jerusalem. This infuriated Paul and caused a rift in his relationship with John Mark. Later, when Paul began his second missionary journey, in A.D. 49, Barnabas again wanted to take John Mark, but Paul adamantly refused. So intense was this disagreement that Barnabas and Paul parted ways. Paul selected Silas as his new traveling companion while Barnabas joined with John Mark and departed to Cyprus.[8]

Disappearing into Cyprus, John Mark is not heard of again for about ten years. When he reemerges on the stage of biblical history, around A.D. 60, he is living with the Christian community in Rome.

John Mark in Rome

When or why John Mark came to Rome is not certain. One of the possible reasons can be found in 2 Timothy 4:11. If the traditional authorship and date of this epistle is accepted, then Paul wrote this epistle while he was a prisoner in Rome, near the close of his life. Feeling deep loneliness and in need of assistance, Paul writes, "Only Luke is with me. Pick up Mark and bring him with you, for he is useful to me for service."[9]

That the "Mark" referred to by Paul is John Mark is fairly certain, due to their previous association. Paul's statement also suggests that somewhere along the way, Paul and John Mark had been reconciled, their friendship rekindled, and that Paul finds Mark "useful to me for service." Thus, John Mark could have initially come to Rome at the urging of the Apostle Paul during the early 60s A.D.

Another biblical reference to John Mark's presence in Rome is found in 1 Peter 5:13. At the close of this epistle, written by Peter toward the end of his life, the apostle writes, "She who is in Babylon [code name for Rome], chosen together with you, sends you greetings, and so does my son, Mark." Now, it is true that many men in Peter's day were named Mark. But given evidence from Paul that John Mark was indeed in Rome, coupled with the writing of Papias, which we will soon explore, Peter's reference to Mark is almost certainly referring to John Mark. Thus, within the pages of the New Testament is strong evidence that John Mark was living in Rome prior to the Neronian persecution in A.D. 64, and that he was in a working relationship with both Peter and Paul.

The Testimony of Papias

Now let us look outside the pages of the New Testament to the writings of one of the earliest Christians, a man by the name of Papias. Papias was likely born around A.D. 60, thirty years after the death of Jesus and near the exact time of the composition of the first Gospel, the Gospel of Mark. By A.D. 130 Papias was the elderly bishop of Hierapolis, which is in modern Turkey, just a few miles northeast of ancient Colossae and Laodicea.

Papias wrote a five-volume commentary on the sayings of Jesus, titled *Exegeses of the Logia of the Lord*. Though this literary work has been tragically lost to history, it was extensively quoted by the early Church fathers from the mid-second century to the mid-fourth century, and from Palestine to Gaul. Papias's recollections were particularly quoted in the writings of Irenaeus of Lyons (A.D. 130–200) and Eusebius of Caesarea, the father of Church history (A.D. 260–340). In reference to the authorship of the Gospel of Mark, Eusebius directly quotes Papias:

> And the Elder said this also: *"Mark having become the interpreter of Peter, wrote down accurately whatever he remembered of the things said and done by the Lord, but not however in order."* For neither did he hear the Lord, nor did he follow him, but afterwards, as I said, Peter, who adapted his teachings to the needs of his hearers, but not as though he were drawing up a connected account of the Lord's oracles. So then Mark made no mistake in thus recording some things just as he remembered them. For he took forethought for one thing, not to omit any of the things that he had heard nor to state them falsely.[10]

In the earliest existing record concerning the authorship of the Gospel of Mark, Papias is clear that the Gospel was written by a man named Mark, who was Peter's personal secretary and who based a portion of the Gospel on what he learned and heard from Peter. Papias's statement was accepted as true by Irenaeus, the Muratorian Canon, Clement of Alexandria, Tertullian, Origen, Jerome, and Eusebius. Each of these Church fathers likewise assumed that this "Mark" was John Mark of Jerusalem.[11]

Impetus for Writing a Gospel

What was the concurrence of events that caused John Mark to begin to write his treatise on the life of Jesus and the disciples who followed him? Perhaps he had many reasons. However, it is likely that the dominant reason was the advent of the Neronian persecution and the probable martyrdom of both Peter and Paul.

In July of A.D. 64, a fire broke out in Rome in the cluttered market near the Circus Maximus. Raging out of control for more than a week, it greatly damaged ten of the fourteen wards of Rome. A rumor rapidly spread that the fire had been covertly ordered by the deranged emperor Nero, in order to clear inner-city land for new and extravagant buildings he wished to erect. Faced with this accusation, Nero blamed the fire on a small religious "cult" called Christians. Tacitus, the Roman historian, tells of the grisly result:

> Neither human resources, nor imperial munificence, nor appeasement of the gods, eliminated sinister suspicions that the fire had been instigated. To suppress this rumor, Nero fabricated scapegoats—and punished with every refinement the notoriously depraved Christians (as they were popularly called). . . . First, Nero had self-acknowledged Christians arrested. Then, on their information, large numbers of others were condemned—not so much for incendiarism as for their anti-social tendencies. Their deaths were made farcical. Dressed in wild animals' skins, they were torn to pieces by dogs, or crucified, or made into torches to be ignited after dark as substitutes for daylight. Nero provided his Gardens for the spectacle, and exhibited displays in the Circus, at which he mingled in the crowd—or stood in a chariot, dressed as a charioteer. Despite their guilt as Christians, and the ruthless punishment it deserved, the victims were pitied. For it was felt that they were being sacrificed to one man's brutality rather than to the national interest.[12]

During the Neronian persecution and its extended aftermath, it is likely that both Peter and Paul suffered martyrdom. The First Epistle of Clement, Bishop of Rome, to the church in Corinth was written ca. A.D. 95, and is the first known document to allude to Peter suffering martyrdom in Rome: "Let us set before our eyes the good apostle Peter, who, through unrighteous envy, endured not one or two, but numerous labors, and having suffered martyrdom departed to the place of glory due him."[13]

It is, however, Tertullian (ca. A.D. 155–222) writing around A.D. 200, who is the first to specifically state that Peter died during Nero's persecution:

> Examine your records. There you will find that Nero was the first that persecuted this doctrine, particularly then when after subduing all the east, he exercised his cruelty against all at Rome. We glory in having such a man the leader in our punishment. For whoever knows him can understand that nothing was condemned by Nero unless it was something of great excellence. Thus publicly announcing himself as the first among God's chief enemies, he was led on to the slaughter of the apostles. It is, therefore, recorded that Paul was beheaded in Rome itself, and that Peter likewise was crucified under Nero.[14]

Later it was Origen (ca. A.D. 185–254) who elaborated on Peter's death by saying, "At last, having arrived in Rome, he [Peter] was crucified head downwards, having himself requested that he might so suffer."[15]

Finally, the Chronicon of Eusebius (Armenian version) states that the martyrdom of Peter took place in the thirteenth year of Nero's reign, or A.D. 67–68.[16]

Faced with the increasing loss of eyewitnesses to the life of Christ, and with the tragedy of the deaths of Peter and Paul, it became increasingly pressing that someone write a treatise that would accomplish two things:

1) Preserve the teachings and events in the life of Jesus, and

2) Give comfort and assistance to Christians suffering persecution in Rome and other parts of the Christian world.

John Mark of Jerusalem accepted this responsibility. And what better qualified person could have done so in an age when first-generation Christians were now scarce and eyewitnesses to the life of Jesus were possibly nonexistent? John Mark possessed at least the following three credentials for writing such a treatise:

1) He had grown up in the very first Christian community in Jerusalem.

2) He had traveled and worked with Paul, Barnabas, and Peter.

3) He had the literary skills and the experiential knowledge to undertake such a task.

What kind of treatise on the life and teaching of Jesus would John Mark write? What would he use as his sources? How would he craft such a document? What themes would he emphasize? What writing style would he employ? His task would not be easy.

The Writing of the First Gospel

New Testament scholars are nearly unanimous today in their opinion that the first Gospel to be written was the Gospel of Mark. It was likely written ten to fifteen years before the Gospels of Matthew and Luke, and was used as a major source and model for their later compositions. Yet when John Mark began to write his treatise, there was no existing form of literature called a *gospel*. Indeed, John Mark not only wrote a treatise, he created a whole new form, or literary genre.

It is important for modern readers to understand what a gospel *is* and *is not*. A two-thousand-year-old New Testament Gospel is not a modern biography. The writers of the Gospels were not interested in presenting the life of Jesus in the way a present-day biographer would, giving a detailed description of every facet and every chapter of Jesus' life. Rather, the Gospel writers simply chose selected moments in Jesus' life that they felt had great theological importance and interest for their specific communities of faith. As an illustration, a modern biographer would go to great pains to tell us much about Jesus' parents, his brothers and sisters, his education, and major developmental factors of his childhood, adolescence, and young adulthood. Yet we know very little about the life of Jesus until the beginning of his public ministry at the age of thirty. Thus, the Gospels are not biography according to the modern understanding of the word.

The New Testament Gospels, while revealing historical truth, are also not written like modern history books. Papias is very clear in saying that Mark was not particularly concerned with exact and correct chronology when he wrote the Gospel of Mark. In fact, comparing the chronologies of the Gospel of Mark and the Gospel of John is likely to cause confusion. Mark creates a public ministry that lasted approximately eighteen months and took place primarily in Galilee. John paints a public ministry extending up to three years, with significant time spent in Judea. A reader with modern expectations will wonder, "Which writer is correct?" The simple fact is that for the ancient reader, correct chronology and the development of extensive historical background was not as important as it is today. Though historically true in their content, the Gospels were not intended to be like today's history books.

So, then, what is a Gospel? While the analogy is not totally adequate, I believe that a Gospel is most like a historical drama produced on a theater stage. For instance, if I were to write and produce a historically accurate play of the life of George Washington, I would not have the luxury of conveying to the audience everything I know about the life of George Washington. Rather, I would have to choose specific and crucial scenes from Washington's life, and develop them on the stage using selected characters and historically accurate narrative or script.

I would also have to decide where to begin—with Washington's birth? his marriage? the Revolutionary War? his presidency? I would have to select which highly charged moment I must build the play toward in order to bring the drama to inspiring conclusion and denouement—Washington's defeat of the British? the completion of his presidency? his return to Mt. Vernon? his death and the tearful tribute of a grateful nation?

In addition, when reviewing the thousands of Washington's friends and relations, I would have to choose which relationships I would allow on the theater stage and how each character would be used to carry along the story. Certainly they must be important characters or unusually interesting personalities, for me to allow them precious time in a two-hour play.

Those same situations and literary dynamics were true for John Mark when he sat down to write about Jesus. He had technological and material limitations, as compared to today's writers. He did not have a laptop computer. He did not have reams of paper and printing presses. John Mark's Gospel needed to be short, succinct, and dramatic. It could spotlight only the crucial events in the life of Jesus. He did not have the space for or luxury of a history or biography as we know them today. John Mark invented a succinct and dramatic new literary genre.

Sources for a Gospel

Another important question concerning John Mark's Gospel is, "Where did he get his information?" In sharp contrast to my ability to pursue research on the life of George Washington, John Mark had no libraries, Internet search engines, or even one comprehensive book with which to research the life of Jesus. Where was data on Jesus' life to be obtained?

John Mark's first source was his own memory, and perhaps his own written notes. This is what New Testament scholars call "oral tradition." For years John Mark had been listening to the stories of his mother, Mary, as well as the recollections and discussions of Paul, Barnabas, Peter, Silas, and hundreds of other anonymous Christians. Though John Mark had no personal memories of Jesus, he had talked with many—such as Peter—who had talked and walked with Jesus of Nazareth.

Second, New Testament scholars are uniform in their opinion that John Mark did have before him short written accounts that had been composed by many Christians over a thirty-five-year period. Perhaps he had a short written description of the feeding of the five thousand or another written collection of some of the teachings of Jesus. None of these written fragments had ever been put into a unified "life of Jesus." But they were valuable sources of information.

As I think of John Mark collecting oral and written sources on the life of Jesus and attempting to arrange them into a coherent story, I am reminded of my Grandmother Walker. Callie Walker lived on the remote, arid plains of northeastern Colorado, where her husband, Eddie Walker, had been a rancher before his death. This region of the United States has some of the hottest summers and harshest winters. All during the summer months, my eighty-year-old grandmother would collect baskets full of scrap cloth and material from her sewing club. Then during the winter months, when she would be cooped up indoors by fierce blizzards, she would make patchwork quilts.

Sorting through the baskets of colored cloth, she would choose the fragments that she liked best. Then she would sit down on the floor and arrange the various pieces of material into some attractive and harmonious form. Scattered and diverse pieces of cloth became beautiful and colorful patchwork quilts. Today, each of my children has such a quilt by which to remember their great-grandmother.

In a sense, the Gospel of Mark is a patchwork quilt. John Mark had to decide which fragments of Jesus' life were accurate and which were questionable and fanciful. He had to decide which stories were the most important and crucial to the life and teachings of Jesus. He also had to choose the stories and teachings that would best support and develop the themes he wanted to emphasize. His work is not a history or a biography but a historical drama of scenes patched together with purpose, planning, direction, thematic intention, and artistry.

Gospel Themes

John Mark could not address every theological issue that Jesus dealt with or relate every sermon that Jesus preached. John Mark had to ask: "What issues are my fellow Christians in Rome dealing with? How can this written account help them? What crucial events in the life of Jesus can bring them both guidance and good news in the midst of difficult times?" We must always remind ourselves that John Mark was not a historian writing for Christians living two thousand years in the future. He was a Christian pastor writing to his specific faith community, which had pressing needs to be addressed.

Though many themes are presented in the Gospel of Mark, *a dominant theme that this present book focuses on is the theme of the struggle of Christian discipleship.* John Mark looked at his fellow Christians in Rome in the midst of the Neronian persecution, and realized that to be a Christian is a most difficult struggle. Many had seen loved ones tortured and killed because they would not renounce their faith. Others were dealing with the gnawing guilt they felt for renouncing their faith—shouting, "I do not believe in Jesus Christ"—in order to protect their families and survive for another day. Faced with such difficult times and events, John Mark decided to develop as a primary theme the idea that it is only through struggle and personal failure that we grow stronger in our faith and in our understanding of Jesus. To develop his theme, John Mark quite naturally chose a character that he knew well—a character whose life most naturally displayed this theme of growing through failure—and brought this person center stage. The character was, of course, Simon Peter.

The Character of Peter and Discipleship

Referring to Simon Peter in the Gospel of Mark, the New Testament scholar Ernest Best states: "If a writer wishes to talk about discipleship using men as examples, there are two obvious approaches. He may either set forward a series of examples of good discipleship with the implication that these examples should be followed or he may instruct through the failures of his examples. Mark chose the latter course."[17]

In so doing, Mark chose Simon Peter as an example of one who had struggled and failed but through his struggles grew stronger. Some scholars have concluded that by doing so, Mark has painted a *negative* portrait of Peter. Hardly so. Rather, what Mark has painted is a *human* portrait of Peter, someone with whom we can easily identify and gain courage and understanding that through our failures, our bad attitudes, our narrow-mindedness, and our sinful natures, God can still make us into strong and useful Christians.

It is likely that John Mark took this character perspective because Peter himself used this confessional approach. Some of the greatest preachers and teachers of the Christian faith were people who have openly shared their personal struggles and have shown how God worked through their failures to make them stronger. Peter is perfect to portray such a character because he was indeed that transparent and confessional character in real life.

By portraying Peter as the epitome of the struggling disciple, John Mark moves one step further, in that he creates for future New Testament writers a character that is historically based, "bigger than life," and a representative figure of Christian discipleship. The esteemed New Testament scholar Raymond E. Brown wrote: "One must keep in mind that Peter may have representative value for Mark, so that he is not to be considered only as an individual. For instance, Mark may think of Peter as a representative of the disciple or of discipleship. . . . Peter may also be the lesson *par excellence* for Christians as to the demands of discipleship upon them."[18]

The importance of this is to see that in later writings of the New Testament, the writers of which had knowledge of Mark's Gospel—the Gospel of Matthew, the Gospel of Luke, the Acts of the Apostles, and possibly the Gospel of John—this representative character of Peter carries over into their writing. Just as Peter symbolizes the struggling Christian disciple in Mark, so the writer of Matthew adopts this same characterization in his Gospel when it is written ten to fifteen years later. Thus, the Apostle Peter—far more than just being his singular historical self in the unified Gospel presentation—is the representative par excellence of the Christian disciple who learns through failure and weakness.

In summation, ample evidence exists to believe that John Mark of Jerusalem is the voice behind the writing of the Gospel of Mark. Owing to the impact of the Neronian persecution, one of John Mark's dominant themes is that it is only through struggle and failure that the mature character of the Christian disciple is formed. To develop this theme, John Mark chose the figure of Simon Peter to portray the role of the disciple who fails, learns from his mistakes, and grows to become the "Prince of the Apostles."

Notes

Introduction

1. Fred Hoyle. *Into Deepest Space* (New York: Harper and Row Publishers, 1974).
2. Herman Melville. Source unknown.
3. Theodore Roosevelt. *The Strenuous Life,* The Works of Theodore Roosevelt, national ed., vol. 13, 1926, 510.
4. Ernest Hemingway. *A Farewell to Arms* (New York: Charles Scribner's Sons, 1929), 249.

Chapter 1

1. Luke 1:36 states that Mary, the mother of Jesus, and Elizabeth, the mother of John the Baptist, were "relatives." It is most likely that they were cousins. Though Elizabeth was much older than Mary, they both were pregnant with their firstborn children at the same time. Luke 1:26 intimates that John was six months older than Jesus. What relationship Jesus had with John as the two boys grew into manhood is unknown.
2. Augustine of Hippo. *Confessions,* 1.1.1.
3. Bob Kall. As quoted in *The Book of Positive Quotations,* ed. John Cook (Minneapolis: Fairview Press, 1997, rpt), 290.
4. Antoine de Saint-Exupéry. *Flight to Arras* (New York: Regnal and Hitchcock, 1942), 22.
5. Elton Trueblood. *Confronting Christ* (Waco, Tex.: Word Books, 1960), 21.

Chapter 2

1. James F. Strange and Hershel Shanks. "Has the House Where Jesus Stayed in Capernaum Been Found?" *Biblical Archaeology Review,* November–December 1982, 26.
2. Albert Schweitzer. *The Quest of the Historical Jesus* (Minneapolis: Fortress Press, 2001), 487.
3. Blaise Pascal. *Pensees,* trans. W. F. Trotter (New York: Modern Library, 1941), no. 229, 73-82.
4. Søren Kierkegaard. *Journals,* 1850.
5. D. Elton Trueblood. *A Place to Stand* (New York: Harper and Row, 1969), 60.
6. Pascal. As quoted by John Lukacs, in *The Duel* (New York: Ticknor and Fields, 1990), 187.
7. Dr. Samuel Johnson. *The History of Rasselas, Prince of Abissinia,* D. J. Enright, ed. (New York: Penguin Classics, 1988), ch. 6, 52.
8. Joseph Conrad. *Victory: An Island Tale,* ed. John Batchelor (Oxford: Oxford University Press, 1996), part IV, ch. 14.

Chapter 3

1. Mark 1:23-31, 40-42; Mark 2:1-12; Mark 3:1-6.
2. William Cowper. *Olney Hymns,* 35.
3. Elbert Hubbard. *The Notebook of Elbert Hubbard* (New York: Wm. B. Wise, 1927).
4. Charles H. Spurgeon. As quoted in *A Treasury of Quotations on Christian Themes,* comp. Carroll E. Simcox (New York: The Seabury Press, 1975), 163.
5. C. S. Lewis. *God in the Dock* (Grand Rapids, Mich.: W. B. Eerdmans Publishing Company, 1970), 29.
6. Thomas Merton. *Life and Holiness* (New York: Doubleday, Image Books, 1963).

Chapter 4

1. Josephus, *War of the Jews,* book II, chapter V. Josephus, *Antiquities of the Jews,* book VII, chapter X. Peter Richardson, *Herod* (Columbia: University of South Carolina Press, 1996), 23.
2. Frank Stagg. *The Broadman Bible Commentary,* "Matthew," vol. 8 (Nashville: Broadman Press, 1969), 164.
3. Eduard Schweizer. *The Good News according to Matthew,* (Atlanta: John Knox Press, 1975), 322.
4. Paul Tournier. *A Place for You* (New York: Harper and Row, 1968), 162.
5. Judith Viorst. *Necessary Losses* (New York: Simon and Schuster, 1986), 263.
6. Harold Kushner. *When All You've Ever Wanted Isn't Enough* (New York: Simon and Schuster, 1986), 132.
7. Gene Owens. Quote from an unpublished sermon delivered at the First Baptist Church of Monroe, North Carolina, February 1985.
8. Eva Young. *Reader's Digest,* November 1987, 80.
9. Mark Twain. *Pudd'nhead Wilson,* (New York: Bantam Books, 1984), 12.
10. Thomas R. Kelly. *A Testament of Devotion* (New York: Harper and Row, 1941), 49.

Chapter 5

1. Blaise Pascal. *Pensees,* trans. W. F. Trotter (New York: Macmillan, 1969, rpt), 403.
2. Mark Twain. As quoted by Floyd Thatcher, address at Furman University, April 3, 1987.
3. Robert J. Havighurst. *Developmental Tasks and Education* (New York: David McKay, 1974), 6-7.
4. William Barclay. The Daily Bible Study Series. *The Gospel of John,* vol. 1 (Philadelphia: Westminster Press, 1975, rev. ed.), 132-133.
5. Grady Nutt. Chapel address at the Southern Baptist Theological Seminary, Louisville, Ky., May 1981.
6. John Claypool. *The Preaching Event* (Waco, Tex.: Word Books, 1980), 108.

Chapter 6

1. Luke 4:16-30.
2. Dietrich Bonhoeffer. *The Cost of Discipleship* (New York: Macmillan Company, 1937, 1961), 13.
3. Eberhard Bethge. *Dietrich Bonhoeffer* (New York: Harper and Row, 1970), 628-631, 655-656, 684-686, 730, 830. Dallas M. Roark. *Dietrich Bonhoeffer* (Waco, Tex.: Word Books, 1972), 13-25.
4. Bonhoeffer. *The Cost of Discipleship* (New York: Macmillan Company, 1937, 1961), 79.
5. Bonhoeffer. *Das Zeugnis eines Boten,* ed. Visser 't Hooft, Geneva, 1945, 46-47.
6. Bonhoeffer. *The Cost of Discipleship* (New York: Macmillan Company, 1937, 1961), 31.
7. Bonhoeffer. *The Cost of Discipleship* (New York: Macmillan Company, 1937, 1961), 43.
8. Mark Twain. As quoted by Carroll E. Simcox, *A Treasury of Quotations on Christian Themes* (New York: Seabury Press, 1975), 7.
9. Martin Luther King Jr. As quoted by Stephen B. Oates, *Let the Trumpet Sound: The Life of Martin Luther King Jr.* (New York: New American Library, 1982), 455.

Chapter 7

1. Walter Bauer, William F. Arndt, and F. Wilbur Gingrich. *A Greek-English Lexicon of the New Testament and Other Early Christian Literature,* 4th ed. (Chicago: University of Chicago Press, 1957) 580.
2. "Journey by Night" attributed to Alfred Noyes. Source unknown.
3. G. B. Caird. *Saint Luke,* ed. D. E. Nineham, The Pelican New Testament Commentaries (New York: Penguin Books, 1963), 133. D. E. Nineham, *Saint Mark,* The Pelican New Testament Commentaries (New York: Penguin Books, 1963), 236. Vincent Taylor, *The Gospel According to St. Mark* (New York: St. Martins Press, 1966), 390. Lionel Koppman, *Sukkot,* ed. William H. Gentz, The Dictionary of Bible and Religion (Nashville: Abingdon Press, 1986), 1005.
4. C. S. Lewis. As quoted in *Reader's Digest,* vol. 132, no. 789 (January 1988), 117.
5. Thomas à Kempis. *The Imitation of Christ,* book 4, chapter 15.
6. Joseph H. Gilmore. "He Leadeth Me! O Blessed Thought" (1834–1918), *Baptist Hymnal* (Nashville: Convention Press, 1991), 52.

Chapter 8

1. The writer of Matthew would later expand Mark's succinct version of Peter's question for the sake of clarity and emphasis: "Behold we have left everything and followed you; *what then will there be for us?*" [italics mine].
2. This sonnet is attributed to Francis Xavier. The person who later formed a seventeenth-century Latin hymn based on the sonnet is unknown. Edward Caswall

derived an English translation from the Latin hymn in 1849. In 1954 Jane Marshall used Caswall's translation to provide the text for her choral anthem *My Eternal King* (New York: Carl Fischer, 1954). It is the text of Marshall's anthem that is presently quoted.

3. Horace Mann. As quoted in Carrol E.Simcox, *A Treasury of Quotations on Christian Themes* (New York: Seabury Press, 1975), 176.

4. August Strindberg. *Miss Julie* (New York: Avon, 1965), preface.

5. Fyodor Dostoevksy. *The Diary of a Writer* (New York: Charles Scribner's Sons, 1949), January 3.

6. Ignatius Loyola. *Prayer for Generosity,* as quoted in *The Macmillan Dictionary of Quotations* (New York: Macmillan Publishing Company, 1987), 487.

7. Paul Tournier. *A Place for You* (New York: Harper and Row, 1968), 149.

Chapter 9

1. David Hill. *The Gospel of Matthew,* ed. David Hill, New Century Bible (London: Oliphants, 1975), 277.

2. Eduard Schweizer. *The Good News According to Matthew* (Atlanta: John Knox Press, 1975), 377.

3. C. S. Lewis. "On Forgiveness," in *The Weight of Glory* (New York: Macmillan Company, 1949), 124-125.

4. William Least Heat-Moon. *Columbus in the Americas* (Hoboken, N.J.: John Wiley and Sons, 2002), viii, 53, 66, 113-114.

5. William Barclay. *Luke,* The Daily Bible Study (Philadelphia: Westminster Press, 1954), 14.

6. *The Quarterly Review,* January–March 1982, vol. 42, no. 2, 79.

7. William Blake. "To the Deists," in *Jerusalem* (New York: Holt, Rinehart and Winston, 1970), 405-407.

8. Henry Ward Beecher. *Life Thoughts Gathered from the Extemporaneous Discourses* (Boston: Philips, Sampson, and Company, 1859).

Chapter 10

1. Joachim Jeremias. *Jerusalem in the Time of Jesus* (Philadelphia: Fortress Press, 1962, 1969), 83-84. Philip J. King, "Jerusalem," in *Anchor Bible Dictionary,* ed. David N. Freedman (New York: Doubleday and Company, 1992), vol. 3, 753.

2. The Synoptic Gospels place Jesus' demonstration in the Temple following his triumphal entry into Jerusalem and shortly before his arrest (Matthew 21:12-13, Mark 11:15-17, Luke 19:45-46). The Gospel of John, however, depicts this scene near the beginning of Jesus' ministry (John 2:13-17). The synoptic chronology is probably correct. See Raymond E. Brown, *The Gospel According to John (I–XII),* vol. 1, The Anchor Bible (New York: Doubleday and Company, 1966), 117-118.

3. Raymond E. Brown. *The Death of the Messiah,* vol. 1 (New York: Doubleday and Company), 706-707.

4. Matthew 26:17-20, Mark 14:12-17, Luke 22:7-14. Passover and the Feast of Unleavened Bread were originally two separate festivals. However, by the time of Jesus, the two festivals had been combined. The Passover–Unleavened Bread festival began with the observance of the Passover meal. The festival lasted for seven days.

5. Peter and John are specifically mentioned in Luke 22:8.

6. Brown. *The Gospel According to John,* vol. 2, The Anchor Bible (New York: Doubleday and Company, 1966), 564.

7. Albert Schweitzer. *Pulpit Helps, June 1982.*

8. Billy Graham. Source unknown.

9. Erich Fromm. *The Art of Loving* (New York: Harper and Row, 1956), 24.

10. Friedrich Nietzsche. "On the Great Longing," in *Thus Spoke Zarathustra,* ed. Walter Kaufman (New York: Viking Press, 1966), 3.

11. Albert Einstein. "The World as I See It," in *Ideas and Opinions,* ed. Sonja Bargmann (New York: Crown Publishing Company, 1954), 8.

Chapter 11

1. Thomas Fuller. *Gnomologia: Adagies and Proverbs,* (1732), no. 1729.

2. Thomas Corneille. "The Cid," in *Six Plays by Corneille and Racine,* ed. Paul Landis (New York: Random House, 1959), 2.6.

3. Pat Conroy. *The Prince of Tides* (Boston: Houghton Mifflin Company, 1986), 128.

4. Friedrich Nietzsche. *The Gay Science,* trans. Walter Kaufmann (New York: Vintage Books, 1974), 28.

5. Lord Byron. "Dedication," in *Don Juan* (New York: Macmillan Company, 1927), st. 53.

6. Dag Hammarskjöld. *Markings,* ed. W. H. Auden (New York: Alfred Knopf, 1964), 45.

7. Leslie D. Weatherhead. *The Christian Agnostic* (Nashville: Abingdon Press, 1965), 219.

8. Brother Lawrence. *The Practice of the Presence of God* (New York: Spire Books, 1958), 50.

9. Thomas R. Kelly. *A Testament of Devotion* (New York: Harper and Row, 1941), 61

Chapter 12

1. Raymond E. Brown. *The Gospel According to John (XIII–XXI),* vol. 2, The Anchor Bible (New York: Doubleday and Company, 1966), 823.

2. Thomas Merton. *The Seven Storey Mountain* (Garden City, N.J.: Image Books, 1948), 256.

3. C. S. Lewis. As quoted in the foreword of Joy Davidman's *Smoke on the Mountain* (Philadelphia: Westminster Press, 1954).

4. Richard R. Grant. *Vital Christianity,* November 18, 1979, 8.

5. Pierre Teilhard de Chardin. *The Phenomenon of Man* (New York: Harper and Row, 1959), 312.

6. Harold Philby. *New York Times,* December 19, 1967.

7. William Barclay. *Hebrews,* The Daily Study Bible (Philadelphia: Westminster Press, 1975), 120.

8. Elizabeth Barrett Browning, "The Meaning of the Look." As quoted in *The Life of Jesus in World Poetry,* eds. Robert Atwan, George Dardess, Peggy Rosenthal (New York: Oxford University Press, 1998), 422.

Chapter 13

1. William Barclay. The Daily Bible Study Series, *The Gospel of John,* vol. 2, rev. ed. (Philadelphia: Westminster Press, 1975) 267. George Beasley-Murray. Word Biblical Commentary, *John,* vol. 36 (Waco, Tex.: Word, 1987), 371-372.

2. Philippians 3:21, 1 Corinthians 15:44.

3. F. F. Bruce, *Paul and Jesus* (Grand Rapids, Mich.: Baker Book House, 1974), 54.

4. Henri Nouwen, *Out of Solitude: Three Meditations on the Christian Life* (Notre Dame, Ind.: Ave Maria Press, 1974), 59-60.

5. R. S. Thomas, "The Answer" from *Frequencies* (London: Macmillan, 1978).

6. Martin Luther King Jr. As quoted in *Reader's Digest,* vol. 132, no. 789 (January 1988), 117.

7. C. S. Lewis, *Mere Christianity* (New York: Macmillan, 1952), 120.

8. John Greenleaf Whittier, "The Meeting." As quoted in *Library of World Poetry,* ed. William Cullen Bryant (New York: Avenel Books, 1980), 287.

Chapter 14

1. Glenn Tinder. "From the Ends of the Earth," in *The Best Christian Writing 2000,* ed. John Wilson (San Francisco: HarperSanFrancisco, 2000), 238-239, 241.

2. Ibid., 248-249.

3. Lewis Smedes. *Forgive and Forget: Healing the Hurts We Don't Deserve* (San Francisco: Harper and Row, 1984), 71, 77.

4. C. S. Lewis. *Letters of C. S. Lewis,* ed. W. H. Lewis (New York: Harcourt Brace Jovanovich, 1966), 230.

5. Dag Hammarskjöld. *Markings,* trans. Leif Sjoberg and W. H. Auden (New York: Alfred Knopf, 1964), 124.

6. Lewis. *Letters of C. S. Lewis,* ed. W. H. Lewis (New York: Harcourt Brace Jovanovich, 1966), 67.

7. L. A. Rochefoucauld. *Moral Maxims* (Newark, Del.: University of Delaware Press, 2002), 116.

Chapter 15

1. Acts 3:2 and Acts 4:22.
2. Henri J. M. Nouwen. *Out of Solitude* (Notre Dame, Ind.: Ave Maria Press, 1974), 34, 41.
3. Ernst Haenchen. *The Acts of the Apostles: A Commentary* (Philadelphia: Westminster Press, 1965, 1971), 200.
4. Nouwen. *Out of Solitude* (Notre Dame, Ind.: Ave Maria Press, 1974), 56.
5. C. S. Lewis. *Mere Christianity* (New York: Macmillan, 1952), 153.
6. Lewis. "The Efficacy of Prayer," in *The World's Last Night and Other Essays* (New York: Harcourt Brace Jovanovich, 1960), 5.
7. Frank A. Clark. As quoted in "Christian Herald," February 1983, 23.
8. Helen Keller. As quoted in "Christian Herald," December 1975, 30.

Chapter 16

1. The word *Christian* is used only three times in the New Testament: Acts 11:26, Acts 26:28, and 1 Peter 4:16. Acts 11:26 states, ". . . and the disciples were first called Christians in Antioch." The word *Christian* was not first used by Christians to refer to themselves but rather by Jews and Gentiles to identify Christians. Many scholars believe that Roman officials in Antioch first coined the phrase as early as 40–44 B.C. See Malcolm Peel, "Christian," in *Mercer Dictionary of the Bible,* ed. Watson Mills (Macon, Ga.: Mercer University Press, 1990), 142.
2. Ambrose Bierce. *The Devil's Dictionary* (New York: Wordsworth Editions, 1996).
3. Leo Tolstoy, *Anna Karenina,* trans. Constance Garnett (New York: Random House, 1939), 3.9.
4. Friedrich Nietzsche. *Images of Man* (Richmond, Va.: John Knox Press, 1965), 43.
5. Nietzsche. *The Gay Science,* trans. Walter Kaufmann (New York: Vintage Books, 1974), 121
6. Nietzsche. *The Gay Science,* trans. Walter Kaufmann (New York: Vintage Books, 1974), 121-122.
7. Ralph Waldo Emerson. "Letters and Social Aims," in *The Complete Works of Ralph Waldo Emerson* (Boston: Houghton Mifflin, 1917), vol. 8, 96.
8. Alfred Adler. As quoted by Phyllis Bottome, *Alfred Adler: Apostle of Freedom* (New York: G. P. Putnam, 1939), ch. 5.
9. Thomas Paine, *The Age of Reason* (New York: Promethius, 1984), 8.
10. Paul Tillich. As quoted by James W. Fowler, *Becoming Adult, Becoming Christian* (New York: Harper and Row, 1984), 87.

Chapter 17

1. Robert Frost. "Mending Wall," in *The Poetry of Robert Frost,* ed. Edward C. Lathem (New York: Holt, Rinehart and Winston, 1969), 33.
2. Erich Fromm. *The Art of Loving* (New York: Harper and Row, 1956), 47.

3. John F. Kennedy. Letter to the National Conference of Christians and Jews, Washington, D.C., October 10, 1960.
4. Philip Wheelwright. "Fragments," in *Heraclitus* (Princeton, N.J.: Princeton University Press, 1959), 90.
5. Ralph Waldo Emerson. *Journals and Miscellaneous Notebooks* (Cambridge, Mass.: Harvard University Press, 1960-1966), 1831.
6. Brooks Atkinson. "April 29," in *Once Around the Sun* (New York: Harcourt Brace, 1951).

Chapter 18

1. 1 Corinthians 9:5.
2. See Appendix: John Mark's Relationship with the Apostle Peter.
3. Leslie D. Weatherhead. *The Christian Agnostic* (Nashville: Abingdon, 1965), 208.
4. Paul Tournier. *A Place for You* (New York: Harper and Row, 1968), 51.
5. Thomas Merton. *Thoughts in Solitude* (New York: Doubleday Image, 1956), 81.
6. Mary B. C. Slade. "Footsteps of Jesus," in *Baptist Hymnal* (Nashville: Convention Press, 1991), 483.

Appendix

1. The primary source outside of the Bible for information on the life of John Mark comes from Papias, the bishop of Hierapolis in Asia Minor, who lived from A.D. 60 to 130. His writings have not survived in original manuscript form. However, both Irenaeus, the bishop of Lyons (A.D. 130–200), and the father of Church history, Eusebius of Caesarea (A.D. 260–340), quote from his writings. Eusebius states that Papias wrote that John Mark "neither heard the Lord nor followed him." Thus, John Mark would at most have been an infant or a young child at the time of the death of Jesus.
2. Acts 12:1-17.
3. The second-century church historian Hegesippus, a converted Jew, wrote five volumes of "Memoirs," none of which exist today. However, fragments were quoted and preserved by Eusebius of Caesarea (A.D. 260–340). Eusebius quotes Hegesippus as saying that James, the brother of Jesus, was executed by the Sanhedrin in A.D. 62. (Eusebius, *Ecclesiastical History,* ii, 23). For reference to Peter traveling with his wife, see 1 Corinthians 9:5.
4. Acts 9:1-19, 22:1-21, 26:1-23; 2 Corinthians 11:32; Galatians 1:17, 21.
5. Acts 9:1-9, 26-30; Galatians 1:11-24. For John Marks's relationship with Barnabas, see Colossians 4:10.
6. Acts 13:21, 23:3, 23:6; Romans 11:1; Philippians 3:5.
7. Acts 12:25—14:28, Galatians 2:9.
8. Acts 12:25; 13:5, 13; 15:36-41.

9. The authorship of 1 and 2 Timothy is disputed by modern-day scholars. However, the traditional authorship has been attributed to Paul, with 2 Timothy having stronger claims for Pauline authorship than 1 Timothy.

10. Eusebius. *Ecclesiastical History,* 3.39.15.

11. John Drane. *Introducing the New Testament* (Minneapolis: Fortress Press, 2001), 197. Walter A. Elwell and Robert W. Yarbrough. *Encountering the New Testament* (Grand Rapids, Mich.: Baker Press, 1998), 88.

12. Tacitus. *Annals XV,* 36-38.

13. Clement of Rome. *1 Clement* 5.4.

14. Tertullian. As quoted by Walter A. Elwell and Robert W. Yarbrough, *Encountering the New Testament* (Grand Rapids, Mich.: Baker Press, 1998), 364.

15. Origen. As quoted by Eusebius of Caesarea, *Ecclesiastical History,* 3.1.2.

16. A. T. Robertson. *Epochs in the Life of Simon Peter* (New York: Charles Scribner's Sons, 1933; rpt. Baker Book House, 1974), 317-319. Elwell and Yarbrough. Op. cit., 364.

17. Ernest Best. *Following Jesus: Discipleship in the Gospel of Mark,* Journal for the Study of the New Testament, Supplement Series 4, The University of Sheffield, 1981, 12.

18. Raymond E. Brown, Karl P. Donfried, John Reumann, eds. *Peter in the New Testament* (Minneapolis: Augsburg Publishing House / Paulist Press, 1973), 62.